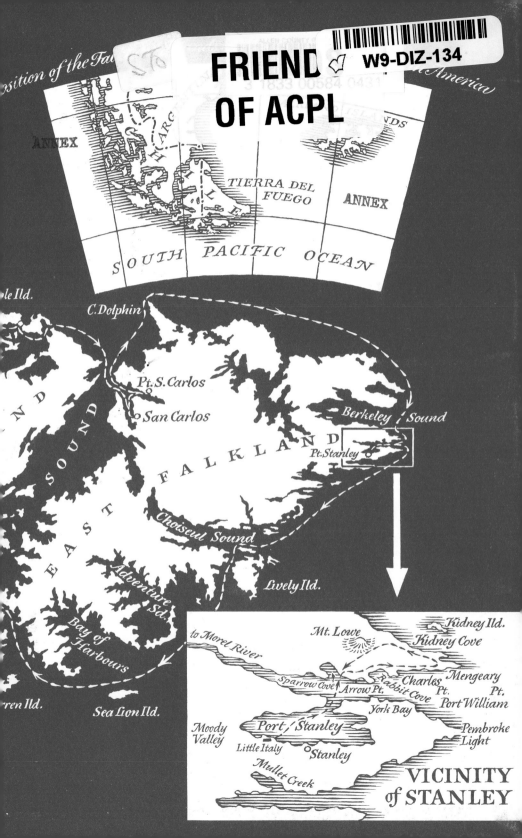

sition of the Fa... ...America

ANNEX

TIERRA DEL
FUEGO

ANNEX

SOUTH PACIFIC OCEAN

le Ild.

C. Dolphin

Pt. S. Carlos

San Carlos

Berkeley Sound

FALKLAND

Pt. Stanley

S O U N D

E A S T

Choiseul Sound

Adventure
Sd.

Lively Ild.

Bay of
Harbours

ren Ild.

Sea Lion Ild.

to Morel River

Mt. Lowe

Kidney Ild.
Kidney Cove

Sparrow Cove

Arrow Pt.

Rabbit Cove

Charles
Pt.

Mengeary
Pt.

Port William

York Bay

Moody
Valley

Port Stanley

Little Italy

Stanley

Pembroke
Light

Mullet Creek

VICINITY
of STANLEY

PENGUIN SUMMER

Photographs by

OLIN SEWALL PETTINGILL, Jr.

PENGUIN
SUMMER

An Adventure With the
Birds of the Falkland Islands

by ELEANOR RICE PETTINGILL

Clarkson N. Potter, Inc./Publisher

NEW YORK

Library of Congress Card Catalog Number: 60-16840

DESIGNED BY HARVEY SATENSTEIN

MANUFACTURED IN THE UNITED STATES OF AMERICA BY

BOOK CRAFTSMEN ASSOCIATES, INC., NEW YORK

First Edition

*Photographic illustrations herein were furnished
by Walt Disney Productions*

1140597

for SEWALL

CONTENTS

Page

Chapter 1: **THE FITZROY** 3

Chapter 2: **COLD** 13

Chapter 3: **CHARLES POINT** 31

Chapter 4: **KIDNEY ISLAND** 43

Chapter 5: **INTERLUDE** 63

Chapter 6: **BACK TO THE PENGUINS** 73

Chapter 7: **AROUND THE CAMP** 87

Chapter 8: **THE SEA-GIRT KINGDOM** 105

Chapter 9: **SUMMER WANES** 159

Chapter 10: **LAST DAYS** 185

ILLUSTRATIONS

Page

The **Fitzroy** provided the only regular means of transportation to the Falkland Islands 2

Lighthouse—Pembroke Light 11

Stanley, the only town in the Falklands and the southernmost capital in the world 12

The **Great Britain**, probably the first propeller-driven iron ship to cross the Atlantic 19

The gentoo penguin colony at Arrow Point; Stanley in the background 20

A gentoo guarding its nest 21

A jackass penguin by the entrance to its underground burrow .. 24

Gentoos celebrate reunion with their mates by trumpeting 30

Gentoos steal diddle-dee twigs from each other to build their nests 33

Gentoos on the beach at Rabbit Cove 36

The author standing by a tussock bog on Kidney Island.......... 38

Rockhopper penguins at their nest 42

A gentoo trumpeting..................................... 46

A rockhopper sitting on its eggs 48

King shags 49

Cliffs at Kidney Island 61

Sewall Pettingill and "Pengy," a pet king penguin 62

A "tussock bog"—Kidney Island 71

Rockhopper nests in the tussock 72

Logger ducks, ungainly flightless birds; unfortunately, the young
     will soon look just like their parents 76

Kelp geese and their young; the all-white bird is the male 77

Kelp geese and young; the original brood of seven has been
     reduced by the depradations of gulls and skuas 78

This handsome sooty albatross was on Kidney Island for three days   80

Jackass penguins on the beach 81

A gentoo parent and its still downy offspring 83

A gentoo and its young 85

Mollymawk and young 86

Black and white oystercatchers 99

Rockhoppers launch themselves into the water from this stone
     ledge 104

Rockhopper penguins, king shags, and mollymawks nest in the
     same areas, generally ignoring each other 108

Rockhopper penguin and young, still in the fuzzy, helpless stage.. 110

Gentoos trumpeting; the young seem unimpressed 112

These rockhoppers are not necessarily angry—they do this all the
     time 118

King shags on their nests 129

King shag and young 138

When rockhopper penguins are old enough to leave the nest, they
     gather in crèches 141

Gentoos in Penguin Valley 145

A skua and its victim, a baby gentoo penguin 147

Young mollymawk 151

"Pettingills Parlour" on New Island 157

A gentoo and its growing young 158

Sewall among the young gentoos 161

A gentoo, returned from the sea, feeds its young 162

During molting, rockhoppers are hungry and irritable 166

A molting rockhopper 167

Sewall on a rocky ledge at Kidney Island 169

Rockhoppers rest precariously on steep rock slopes 174

Mollymawks and rockhoppers 183

Whalebone arch 184

Young gentoos, fascinated, explore the water 188

Young gentoos taking their first dip 189

Eleanor Pettingill 198

PENGUIN SUMMER

The Fitzroy provided the only regular means of transportation to the Falkland Islands

Chapter 1

THE FITZROY

Surrounded by eleven enormous pieces of luggage, I stood on a busy dock beside the gangplank of a small freighter. My husband had already gone aboard, vanishing into an anthill of activity. The decks swarmed with stevedores loading cargo; important-looking people ran about checking lists; passengers and guests clogged the gangplank, tripping over my bags. There were greetings, conversations, directions, commands in English and Spanish, occasionally in French and German. The day was warm, but I shivered, half in excited anticipation of the voyage, half in dread of our remote destination.

The time was October—early spring in Montevideo, Uruguay; the freighter was the *Fitzroy,* about to sail for the Falkland Islands, over a thousand miles away. She was an 840-ton ship, sometimes referred to as a tug, a barge, or a rusty bucket, and she carried mail and passengers to the Falklands once every six weeks—the only regular link between the islands and the outside world.

Dwarfed by a great white luxury liner, she seemed insignificant. Her hull was black and rusty, her superstructure white with orange trim; her single stack was grimy, and her decks a maze of cranes, winches, and hawsers. But she had an air of grace and independence. Perhaps it was a whim on my part, or possibly the instant confidence I felt in her captain, Frederick W. White, so smart in his trim uniform; anyway, I liked the *Fitzroy.* She looked as if she could be trusted in any sea.

The ship was loaded, and when the holds were crammed full and the iron hatches battened down, two small cars were swung

3

aloft and lowered to the aft hatch, and two huge pens of sheep were placed on the forward hatch. After the sheep came five English sparrows, that fluttered about the rigging waiting for a chance to descend to the pens in search of food.

We embarked on the *Fitzroy* on October 17, 1953, twenty years after I had first heard of the Falkland Islands from my husband, Sewall Pettingill, an ornithologist. He had come home from a meeting of the American Ornithologists' Union in a state of high excitement.

"It's the only place in the world where we can live with people and still be near three kinds of penguins," he said.

We hastened to see what we could find out about the Falklands. A map showed them to be a tiny archipelago in the South Atlantic some 300 miles east of the Strait of Magellan and 800 miles north of the Palmer Peninsula of Antarctica. It was the southernmost, and most isolated, of the British Crown Colonies, and its capital and only town was Stanley.

Apart from that there was little enough to learn. There were two main islands, East Falkland and West Falkland, and more than a hundred outlying islets; their total land area was the size of the state of Connecticut. About 2500 people, mostly British or of British descent, lived there, half of them in Stanley. Their occupation was sheep farming, and mutton, consequently, their principal food. Peat was their only fuel and horseback their chief means of transportation. The landscape was rugged and treeless with strange geological phenomena, "rivers of stone," that looked like streams flowing into the sea. It was a cold land over which bitter winds swept continuously. We could find nothing attractive about it, nothing that gave promise of being so. Even the description of the ship by which one reached it was derogatory. But there were penguins, thousands and thousands of them, which gathered on the islands each summer to nest and rear their young; and penguins were what we wanted.

Sewall wrote to the Governor of the Falkland Islands for permission to visit them to study and photograph penguins. The reply granting the request was slow in coming because of the *Fitzroy's* schedule, and before the letter arrived, World War II had begun. We filed it away and forgot it. Meanwhile Sewall photographed other birds in other places: roseate spoonbills in Texas, sage grouse in Wyoming, western grebes in North Dakota,

Alta Mira orioles in Mexico. Some of the film he sold to Walt Disney Productions for the new True-Life Adventure series.

Then one day an idea struck him. "I should think Walt Disney could use some movies of penguins," he said.

Disney, after hearing an enthusiastic description of the Falkland Islands and their penguins, left Sewall speechless with the question, "When are you ready to go?"

We began to plan at once. Although the air age had improved communications elsewhere, the *Fitzroy* was still the only means of carrying mail and passengers to the Falklands, and two months elapsed before our letter to the Governor was answered by a terse note from the office of the Colonial Secretary granting us permission to come and directing us to the London office of the Falkland Islands Company to arrange our transportation. We secured reservations to leave Montevideo in mid-October and return in March.

A second note from the Colonial Secretary's office advised us to bring the kind of clothing we would take for a visit to the United Kingdom—"mainly rough country clothing" and a couple of suits plus dinner dress.

Sewall exploded. "Dinner dress! I won't. . . ."

I added dinner dress to the list I was making.

Next we tried to locate someone in the islands who was interested in birds and natural history. Although ornithologists have friends everywhere in the world, inquiries among Sewall's colleagues drew negative replies or the question, "Just where are the Falkland Islands?" Finally we heard of Mr. Edwin Cawkell, Director of Public Education in the colony and an excellent amateur ornithologist, and wrote to him at once. In his reply he invited us to make his home our headquarters, since living conditions for outsiders were impossible. He advised us to bring all the equipment we would need; to count on buying only food and some extra clothing in Stanley; and not to bother with hides (bird blinds) since the wind would blow them over, and anyway the birds were all tame. This last statement baffled us. We knew penguins were tame, but what about the other birds?

Sewall set about acquiring cameras: two Cine-Kodak Specials for movies; two Leicas, one mounted on a gunstock; two tripods; an assortment of lenses; and a Stroboflash outfit. He also included at the last minute an ancient Graflex which had served him unfailingly on previous expeditions.

I collected the equipment we would need for life outdoors in a country about which I knew nothing except that it was cold, forbidding, and always windy. We unpacked and tested the items that arrived almost daily—sleeping bags, huge ankle-fit boots, wool shirts and socks, windproof jackets, fishermen's raincoats, and underwear—experimental garments of pure orlon fashioned by Munsingwear. We practiced pitching mountain tents in the back yard and firing the special paraffin-burning primus stove on the porch.

At last I felt ready to face anything except—"Except in and around Stanley there are no roads and the only means of traveling overland is on horseback." This sentence from a government pamphlet haunted me. I did not ride horseback.

When our equipment had been shipped to the Disney Studio in Burbank, California, we flew West for two weeks' indoctrination under the guidance of Mr. Erwin Verity, one of the men in charge of True-Life Adventures. We spent hours trying to foresee and prepare for every problem we could possibly encounter in the Falklands—estimating the amount of film we would need, arranging for its disposal once the pictures were taken, providing means of protecting ourselves and the cameras from the elements. Cameras were tested again and again, spare parts were added, and adjustments made. We spent a whole day in the shipping department sorting and repacking under Mr. Verity's watchful eye. We had a great deal of extra equipment—nets, jars, and materials for the preservation of botanical and zoological specimens requested by colleagues. Mr. Verity generously agreed to ship everything, even Sewall's bird gun; but when the dinner jacket appeared he could no longer contain himself.

"Good lord, man! We're sending you to photograph penguins, not to dress like them." We reminded him of the letter from the Colonial Secretary's office, and he yielded; but we could hear him muttering as he left, "Desolation, worst weather in the world, and he needs a dinner jacket."

When everything was packed to be sent ahead by air freight, except our personal luggage and the cameras and lenses which were to be kept with us at all times, Mr. Verity, with a brace of lawyers, produced the contract. I was eager to sign until I read,

"We hereby engage and retain the services of Eleanor Pettingill ... to co-operate with and assist Mr. Pettingill as he may direct." I hesitated. As he may direct! But things had gone too far. Feeling a traitor to my sex, I signed.

The *Fitzroy*, a regular Noah's Ark, carried in addition to the sheep and sparrows an assortment of dogs, cats, chickens, and canaries, and twenty-seven passengers. We had a comfortable cabin on the aft deck, where we could easily set up a camera if we saw a chance to take good photographs. The food was excellent and well-served; there was no sign of scouse, that gastronomic mainstay of southern voyages. The weather was delightful and life was so pleasant that if Captain White had not pointed out the Southern Cross dead ahead, I might have thought we had taken the wrong ship in the wrong direction. A trip to the Falklands on the *Fitzroy* was reputed to be one of the roughest, ruggedest sea voyages in the world.

From the first morning we were followed by birds. Looking through binoculars I saw them everywhere out over the open sea, thousands of them gliding and swooping just above the water. They all looked too much alike for my untutored eye to identify, but Sewall quickly spotted two species of petrels: large brown giant fulmars, and smaller, more delicate black and white Cape pigeons. Both of them were scavengers and kept close to the ship to look for garbage, the fulmars floating casually overhead or diving low to snatch a morsel from the water, and the Cape pigeons passing from side to side keeping pace with the ship. Occasionally a black-browed albatross, or mollymawk, effortlessly circled over us. Sewall said that close to twenty species of petrels and six species of albatrosses occurred regularly along the *Fitzroy's* course.

We picked up some land birds too; it was migration time in the Southern Hemisphere, and we saw two large greenish fly-catchers, a mockingbird, and a song sparrow, probably deflected from their regular South American routes by winds and storms. The mockingbird came aboard the first afternoon, beaten and bedraggled, its plumage soaked with spray. Someone picked it up near the sheep pen and brought it to Sewall. Ornithologists always look at birds as prospective scientific specimens; but this bird's condition was wretched enough to save its life. Sewall wiped it off and put it in our cupboard half-expecting it to die.

Late that evening the first mate brought us a very small sparrow that had struck the glass of the wheelhouse and broken its neck. Heedless of the hour, Sewall dug out his scalpel, corn meal, carbon tetrachloride, cotton, etc. I squeezed into my berth because there was no place else to go, and read a book, ignoring the mess he was making. Early in my married life I had learned that regardless of the awkwardness of the situation, an ornithologist never wastes a specimen. Now and again I leaned across the skinning table to peek at the mockingbird in the cupboard. It seemed to have improved. Next morning it was perky and bright and we knew it must be hungry. When we released it near the sheep pen, it joined the "bread line" with the English sparrows and kept them company for two days. Then it disappeared.

One morning we heard someone cry "Whale" and all but crushed each other trying to get out the narrow cabin door. There were two whales, spouting and playfully rolling over and lifting their tail flukes in the air, indifferent to the ship's passing.

The day before we reached the Falklands someone spotted a school of blackfish—not fish at all, but a kind of porpoise— swimming along behind the ship. Black and glistening, they appeared and disappeared in unison as they overtook us and came alongside; but something disturbed them and they suddenly vanished. Then we saw our first penguin. A passenger shouted and pointed to a small dark object that was porpoising along in and out of the water with incredible speed. Sewall was as surprised as I was. Even when a tousle-headed young man beside me assured us it was a penguin and that was the way they always traveled, we could hardly believe it: two hundred miles from land scarcely seemed the place for a flightless bird.

That morning the wireless operator made contact with the Falklands and cheerfully reported to the lounge that it was snowing in Stanley. This was not news to the other passengers; the weather was always bad there. Next time, they suggested, he might get them some news of people.

At noon we were invited to have drinks in the captain's cabin on the upper deck. From this height the waves seemed as high as houses. They struck the ship from the side and made her roll. Luncheon that day was lively. The wind increased and the *Fitzroy* turned to meet it head on. Climbing up each mountainous wave, she paused on top as if to catch her breath, then pitched forward and plunged down with utter abandon, propeller out of water, vibrating, shaking, rattling.

The passengers staggered into the dining saloon, clinging to the chairs, which fortunately were permanently fastened down. Rails were put up around the tables and the cloths wet down to keep the dishes and silver from sliding. Most of the food stayed in place except the soup, which had a curious way of quietly escaping from the dish before it could be eaten. Thanks to dramamine, all the passengers were on hand.

We had quickly become acquainted with them. They were farm owners, farm managers, employees of the government or the Falkland Islands Company, and their families, returning to the islands from leave abroad. Some of them were native Falklanders—"Kelpers," they called themselves—and others had been born in the United Kingdom. All of them seemed happy to be coming home. We sat in the sun, walked the deck, or played bridge all day; and I began to learn something about life in the islands. Stanley, they told us, was the worst part of it. If we really wanted to see the Falklands, we must go into the "camp"— the camp (from the Spanish *campo,* field) was all the area outside Stanley. But they wondered how we could do it if we did not ride horseback; there was no other way.

The next day an unfamiliar restlessness came over the ship, and in the afternoon there was a noticeable change. After four pleasantly relaxing days, our comfortable little shipboard world was breaking up. On deck a bitter wind chilled us to the bone, and thick clouds obscured the sun. Inside in the lounge, the casual conversations had ceased. Some of the passengers were already in their cabins packing, while others paced about impatiently.

Peering through the windows of the smoking room we saw a faint dark outline through the bank of clouds ahead, the first land we had sighted in five days. As darkness came on, it began to rain. Ahead Pembroke Light flashed; it was the only such beacon in the Falklands and one of the southernmost in the world.

Having packed our luggage we dressed in old but warm clothes and came back to the lounge, prepared to endure with our fellow passengers the interminable last half hour before landing. But when we stepped inside and saw them I changed my mind.

Here we were about to debark at Stanley, the only town in

the remotest colony of the British Empire, on a cold, windy, rainy night; and here they were dressed as if for an evening in London. The first costume to catch my eye was a teal-blue coat with gloves and purse to match and a pretty hat with flowers of blending shades. Up the stairs came a woman in a blue faille suit with an opossum coat flung casually over her shoulders. From her trim French heels to her picture hat she was perfect. A third relaxed in a chair with a fur coat flung over her knees. And here was I, the first American woman to visit the Falklands in ages, a picture of utter shabbiness—hatless, in slacks, and on my feet pink socks and dirty white sneakers. Where were the cashmeres and wool skirts of the past few carefree days? I felt betrayed, and I ran back to the cabin hoping our luggage had not been removed.

When I entered the lounge again not ten minutes later I was dressed, not to match the other women, but at least in my best, with high heels, hat, purse, gloves, a wool suit topped by a thin, bright-red coat. A gentleman, seemingly bound for Piccadilly, approached through the opposite door. He had cast aside the tweeds of his journey and was about to step ashore in a navy blue pin-stripe suit, black bowler hat, yellow gloves, brief case, tan raincoat, and an umbrella—the kind you must take back to the shop to be properly furled if you ever use it, which you never should. It was the only umbrella I saw in the Falklands.

There was little noise or confusion as we drew up to the dimly lighted jetty. The police, customs officer, and doctor came aboard. Friends spotted friends ashore, but with traditional British reserve they waved casually, as if they had been separated only for a day instead of for six months or a year. Although we could see little beyond the rail, someone took the trouble to point out Mr. Cawkell in the group on the jetty.

The wind tugged at my hat and whipped through my thin coat as we went down the gangplank to meet Mr. Cawkell, and I stumbled as my high heels caught between the boards of the jetty. Shadowy figures hurried by, calling good night, and disappeared into the darkness. I caught a glimpse of a woman holding desperately to a picture hat and another of a gentleman, umbrella still furled, striding through the rain. We stowed our bags in a Land-Rover—a kind of jeep—and with Mr. Cawkell atop the luggage in the rear and Sewall and me squeezed beside the driver in the front, we bounced off over the worst roads yet built by man, through the dark town to the Cawkells' house.

Lighthouse—Pembroke Light

Stanley, the only town in the Falklands and the southernmost capital in the world

Chapter 2

COLD

Mrs. Cawkell, a charming red-haired little person, brought us hot tea as we sat by a smoldering peat fire, trying to conceal our chattering teeth and shaking limbs.

Sewall and Edwin Cawkell had begun to talk about birds, as ornithologists do the moment they get together. Mr. Cawkell, a tall dark man in his early forties, began to outline our whole expedition for us. He had a quick and orderly mind and was thoroughly familiar with the birds of the Falklands, where three of the seventeen species of penguins in the world can be found: the gentoo, which stands about thirty inches high and nests on bluffs above the sea; the jackass, somewhat smaller, which nests in underground burrows; and the rockhopper, which nests on cliffs and is sometimes called the jumping-jack, from its strange way of hopping.

Unrolling a detailed map of the islands, Mr. Cawkell pointed out two oval harbors on the northeast side, Port William and Port Stanley, connected by a small strait, the Narrows. Opposite this, on the south side of the inner harbor, lay Stanley. We could spend our first six weeks in the vicinity of Stanley, photographing gentoo penguins on Arrow Point, which jutted out into Port William, and rockhopper penguins on Kidney Island, which lay just outside. We would not need to ride horseback; boats were better, if they were available—though he seemed a little uncertain that they would be.

For early December, he recommended a ten-day trip "around the camp" in the *Fitzroy*. It sounded wonderful to me—I already missed the warm, snug stateroom on the aft deck. Then he and

13

Mrs. Cawkell hoped we would be their guests for the Christmas holidays. After that, he had arranged for us to spend a month on New Island, a privately owned sheep farm in the West, and the best place in the Falklands for birds. By February when the Cawkells left for their six months' holiday in England, we should be able to get along on our own.

"There are dozens of other places that would be marvelous," he told us, "but I've picked the most accessible. You can't afford to go any place where you might be marooned for weeks."

The tea and the fire were warming me, and I had almost forgotten the wind howling outside. I felt drowsy. It might not be so bad, I thought.

But when we went through the icy passage to the bedroom and I slipped between the cold sheets, I was no longer shivering, I was rigid. Then my feet touched a hot water bottle.

If it hadn't been for the magic appearance of a pot of tea on our bedside table and an overwhelming curiosity to see the town by daylight, I should never have left the bed the next morning. A strong wind whipped the small house mercilessly and came in around the window panes. We looked out at the churning, wave-tossed harbor, dull gray hills, and beyond them black and craggy mountains reaching to a sullen sky.

Our room was cold; the bathroom was colder; in the dining room where we ate breakfast, we could see our breath. Rowan, the ten-year-old daughter of our hosts, didn't even look cold.

I was trying to force a spoonful of porridge between chattering teeth when I heard the plop, plop, plop of heavy feet in the passage. A black head with a pointed beak appeared around the door and a great big bird waddled into the room.

"Great Scott, a king penguin!" Sewall said.

The Cawkells were amused. The creature moved closer and rested its beak on the table.

The bird, Edwin told us, a young, full-grown, but not yet highly colored king penguin, had come ashore in Stanley Harbour with its feathers all covered with oil. Edwin cleaned it up and returned it to the water. It landed again and refused to leave. At the moment it was living in the back garden together with the chickens, four cats, and a dog.

"Likes to come in the house, though, whenever he has a

chance," Edwin said. "I feed him at the kitchen table—mutton, or once in a while some mullet. When the tide is high in the afternoon I toss him into the harbor for a swim. Comes right back in about ten minutes."

"He's been here long enough," Mrs. Cawkell said uneasily.

Rowan slipped from her chair. "Come on, Pengy," she said. She approached the bird from behind and grasping it firmly by the flippers, she half carried, half dragged it from the room.

A burst of lively music came from the sitting room. There was no regular radio program during the day, so all sets were left on for special announcements, introduced by a gay theme song. Fresh fruit brought by the *Fitzroy* would be in the shops by noon, the announcer said, and the plane would not fly today. Although there is no air service to the Falklands, one can travel about the islands in a government plane, a Beaver on floats, planes with wheels being impractical because of the scarcity of landing places.

Edwin looked out the window at the weather. "No need wasting radio time to tell us they can't fly today," he said. "Sometimes I think they're all mental."

Putting on layers of sweaters and our heaviest coats we set out to look over the town. The Cawkells' house stood midway in a row of neat one-story wooden dwellings strung along a shelf above the harbor southwest of Stanley. All of them were white with red roofs; all had yards enclosed by white fences or hedges just beginning to show yellow blooms—gorse, imported from Scotland; all had glass porches bright with flowers. In a few front yards daffodils were struggling to raise their heads against the beating wind.

Between the houses and the harbor rose a granite shaft surmounted by a bronze model of an Elizabethan ship, a memorial to the famous Battle of the Falkland Islands in World War I. This section of the town was called Little Italy, possibly because the small houses, the homes of government officials, resembled villas; certainly not because Stanley Harbour could ever be mistaken for the Mediterranean. From the monument there was a good view of the town—red roofs, chimney pots, the spire of a large church; and the water front—jetties, hulks, and a ship.

Between Little Italy and Stanley proper stood Government House, an aggregation of several buildings. There was a unit of

red brick with peaks and gables that might have been transported
from an English village, and another of wood painted white that
might have come straight from Bermuda. Only the lowest wing,
of gray stone, seemed to be in keeping with the rock-strewn
slope behind it. Straight across the front ran a long glass porch,
a conservatory, tying all three parts together. White fences and
gorse outlined the drives, paths, and gardens. Directly in front
of the house was a lone, twisted evergreen tree, mistakenly
referred to as the only tree in the Falklands.

Edwin had instructed us to stop at Government House and
"sign the book," thereby announcing our arrival in the colony.
After that, he assured us, we would receive an invitation to tea,
cocktails, or dinner. I hoped it would come quickly, so that we
could get on with our work: according to protocol, we could
not leave Stanley until we had fulfilled this social obligation. The
Governor, it seemed, was aware of our purpose and anxious to
give all possible aid.

Beyond Government House small cottages, mostly of stone,
lined the narrow streets that left Ross Road and went abruptly
up a steep slope, Sappers Hill, that came as a surprise to me,
since the only photograph of the town I had seen—an aerial
view—had given me the impression it was flat. Sewall remarked
that it looked like Duluth; I suggested Marblehead—in November.
But there was nothing of the youthful bustle of Duluth about it,
or the prissy neatness of Marblehead. Although Stanley was new
even by American standards, there was a feeling of age and
rugged endurance in the weathered wood and crumbling stone
walls.

In the center of town stood the high, red brick cathedral of the
Church of England, and in front of it, in the middle of a small
park, the Whalebone Arch—a curious structure formed from the
jawbones of two whales, and erected by the Falkland Islands
Company in 1933 to commemorate the one hundredth anniversary
of the colony.

We visited the post office and several shops. They were all
cold, but the Falkland Islands Company store, which was housed
in an enormous airplane hangar, was the worst. Only at the
house of the banker, Mr. Ernesto Rowe, where we went to
change our money, did we have a respite—a cup of hot coffee
beside a peat fire that actually burned.

Walking into town with the wind at our backs had been easy, but when we left the shelter of the buildings and headed home, we walked straight into the cruel wind that swept the width of the harbor, and we could hardly keep our footing on the narrow walk along the sea wall. I was blinded by tears before I reached the gorse bushes that banked a flight of stone steps leading to the monument. I'll never go out again, I resolved as I staggered into the Cawkells' house. But it was cold there too; all the windows were open from the top, and the maid was attacking the rugs with a stiff-bristled brush.

My memory of our first days in the Falklands is dominated by the ever present, ever penetrating cold. No matter how many clothes I wore, I shivered and trembled; and I felt even more desperate when I realized that there was really no place to go to be warm. What was even more infuriating, no one else seemed to mind the cold. No one wore parkas, windproof jackets, or snow pants. People dressed just as they would in England, and almost everyone scorned central heating. But I took some comfort in recalling that Sir Ernest Shackleton had been colder in Stanley than in Antarctica.

The cold those first days sapped all my strength. Sewall teased me about my concern for "creature comforts," but he was uncomfortable too. Neurotic like most men, he decided he had leukemia. I laughed, as I always did over his periodic outbreaks of tuberculosis and cancer.

"If I don't have leukemia, why am I always so cold?" he demanded.

The thermometer in our room, registering 46°, answered that question.

There were few birds around Stanley, but we saw some new and exciting ones on our short walks. On the rocky hillside behind the house, I saw a black and white bird, somewhat like a meadowlark, that turned around to display a gorgeous rosy red breast. The ornithologists called it a red-breasted troupial, but in the Falklands it was also known as a starling or a robin red-breast.

Climbing Sappers Hill we flushed Correndera pipits from the thin grass. They were one of the southernmost song birds in the world, Sewall told me, as they rose in the air to give their spring flight songs. But I could not hear them above the wind and could not imagine why he was so excited about the small dull creatures.

On rocky outcrops we saw slender gray birds, obviously fly-catchers, but long-legged ones. They perched on the highest spots, jagged rocks or sprigs of shrubs no more than eight inches above the ground, from which they darted suddenly after minute insects. "Ground-tyrants," Sewall said, "like phoebes on stilts."

There was one very familiar bird—a faded version of an American robin hopping about in the back garden. Because the British robin is quite a different bird from the American robin, Edwin insisted that this was the Falkland thrush. I could always get a rise out of him by calling a Falkland thrush a robin, and we carried on a running argument about it.

Head down, bucking the wind, I saw more of the ground than of birds. Outside the town was sheep pasture, with narrow paths winding among clumps of tough white grass and patches of a low, dark shrub called diddle-dee, one of the few native woody plants of the islands. Mosses and lichens grew profusely over and around the harsh gray rocks. Everywhere the ground seemed damp and squashy. On a level area near the summit of Sappers Hill we found peat cuts and stopped to probe the mucky earth, the color and consistency of chocolate fudge. Here and there blocks of cut peat had been stacked like black igloos. There was plenty of peat around Stanley, Edwin said; the difficulty was getting anyone to cut it.

There were birds around the harbor too. Just off shore big ducks—logger ducks or flightless steamer ducks—with grayish white heads bobbed on the waves and croaked at us as we passed. One pair had boldly appropriated a rusty iron pipe that extended into the water near Government House, and here they rested undisturbed. Even though they could not fly, they were perfectly safe because they were not fit to eat.

The slaughter house on the water front at the eastern edge of town was the gathering place for sea birds—giant fulmars (often called stinkers); kelp gulls, similar to the great black-backed gulls of the Maine coast; dolphin gulls, small, trim gray birds with blood-red feet and bills; and skuas, somber creatures on land, but stunning in flight, transformed by their white wing markings. The birds fed on the offal discharged into the harbor.

We had hardly unpacked our heavy clothing before Edwin Cawkell organized a survey expedition into the camp. I think he wanted to find out how tough we were before he turned us loose on our own. In a drizzling rain and a knife-sharp wind, we set out with Edwin, Rowan, and a young schoolmaster, Stuart Booth, a tall, thin man who was an accomplished hiker and mountaineer.

The *Stockfish,* a sturdy gray boat, the only one available for trips inside the harbor, was waiting for us at the end of a long jetty. We boarded her and clung to the benches in her dark hold while she bucked her way through the Narrows and across Port William to Sparrow Cove. When we got there the rain had turned to snow. We could easily have returned to Stanley and tried another day, but Sewall never postponed anything on account of the weather.

The Great Britain, *first propeller-driven iron ship to cross the Atlantic.*
Queen Victoria *once trod her polished decks*

I looked at the gloomy scene. Stark in the center of Sparrow Cove, in the shadow of a mountain that rose abruptly from the sea, lay the gaunt iron hull of a ship, her rusted masts outlined against the gray, rock-strewn slope. No ghost or shipwreck this, Edwin told us, but the remains of the *Great Britain,* the first iron ship driven by a screw propeller to cross the Atlantic. After years of faithful service carrying colonists to Australia, she had been disabled rounding the Horn and had managed to reach Stanley. The owners' advice was "to take her out and sink her," but the Falklanders towed her to Sparrow Cove and grounded her—ignominiously, I thought—in ten feet of water. There she lay, useless except for the mussels that encrusted her sides. We ate some later and found them delicious.

We climbed a bluff through snow and rain to Arrow Point. Scattered sheep eyed us calmly. I was striding along determinedly, head down, when I heard Sewall call, "There they are!"

The gentoo penguin colony at Arrow Point; Stanley and Mount William
in the background

And there they were—our first penguins, a colony of gentoos, hundreds of black and white birds, a carpet of birds tossed on a bluff above the sea. We hurried toward them, then slowed our steps. I found myself standing beside real live gentoo penguins. I could have reached out and shaken a flipper.

I looked at one closely. Its head, back, and flippers were black; across its head, which was flecked here and there with white feathers, curved a thin band, a white coronet. It lifted its orange beak in my direction, then turned and paddled away on huge orange feet.

The penguins all around us were just as oblivious of us as they were of the beating wind and sleet. They all seemed to be working on little heaps of twigs. They stepped aside as we passed, then returned to their engrossing business of building nests out of diddle-dee. A few of them were sitting on the nests, just like chickens. I had always thought penguins nested standing

A gentoo guarding its nest

up—emperor and king penguins do, Sewall said, but not gentoos.

Rowan was scurrying among the birds. There were lots of eggs, she reported. They were safe here; egging was prohibited in this colony. After the disappearance of a colony near Stanley where eggs had been taken freely for years, especially during "egging week," an annual holiday for children during the height of the laying season, the Government had decided to protect this one. Thousands of eggs were still collected in the camp, but none on Arrow Point. Stuart Booth cynically observed that the shortage of boats protected the eggs more than any conservation law.

Since we could not tarry long, we set off again, Stuart Booth in the lead with long strides, while I came up in the rear, on the run. We followed the shoreline down to a small cove, Rabbit Cove, where a few gentoo penguins rested on a broad white sand beach, and tiny Falkland plovers, much like the semipalmated plovers of the Northern Hemisphere, raced along the edge of the water.

We climbed up to Charles Point, an exposed headland on which, half-buried in sod, stood a small metal hut. We scrambled down a four-foot bank and entered its only door. It was damp and chill and empty inside and the wind blew in the cracks.

"Be sure and fasten the door when you leave," Stuart Booth said cheerfully. "A sheep might wander in and die. Make it awkward for the next fellow."

"When we leave—" I started to say. Then I realized that this was what we were supposed to live in when we came to photograph the gentoo penguins.

"But there's no stove," I said.

"You can use a primus," Edwin said.

"We might just come over every day to photograph, and return to Stanley at night," I suggested.

"Too uncertain in this weather," Edwin said.

I tried one more objection. "What about water? We can't live where there's no water."

Mr. Booth pricked that bubble of hope. "All you have to do to get water is dig a hole," he said, pressing his foot hard on the ground and watching the water ooze around it. "There's a well around here somewhere. When you find it, just scoop out the algae, and it will clear in a few minutes."

Surface water in a sheep pasture! Did he think . . .?

I became resigned. The hut would be better than a tent anyway.

We started off again, laboring up headlands whose jagged points reached like fingers into the sea, and descending to beaches of pure white sand that gleamed even on a dull gray day. The weather changed from snow to hail to sleet, then to rain, with a few bursts of sunshine. On the uplands all was gray. Nothing obscured the view, not a tree or shrub broke the monotony of the rolling gray hills. We marveled when Edwin spotted a pair of brent geese in the bleak pasture—the beautiful brown male and small mottled female blended so perfectly into the landscape that they were all but invisible. We flushed a Paraguayan snipe that was feeding in a tiny rivulet of water, and disturbed a pair of trim winter plovers that must have been nesting. On the beach we met our first black and white oystercatchers, huge shore birds with striking plumage and long bright-red bills. Kelp gulls circled overhead, and many Falkland plovers ran along the shore.

Around noon Mr. Booth allowed us to sit down in a protected niche in the cliffs overlooking a small bay called Kidney Cove. While we lunched on sandwiches and tea, the sun came out and it was almost warm. Below us the clear, churning water swished long brown ribbons of kelp back and forth, making strange abstract patterns against the white sand beneath. Beyond the rocks curved the wide arc of a white beach. Suddenly I felt for the first time the charm of the Falkland Islands—but it vanished quickly in a swirl of snow. Then the sun came out again.

Exhausted, I lay back to rest while the others talked. When we got up to go, I realized I should never have stopped. Every muscle in my body ached.

I followed the others down the steep slope, walking like a doll on stiff legs. On the way we met our first jackass penguins lumbering up the hill. They had black and white striped faces, and pink-rimmed eyes, and were so funny-looking that I laughed out loud.

Mr. Booth stood in the path of one bird and tried to make it turn back. The penguin merely stopped, moved its head slowly from side to side, and eyed him stubbornly.

"Watch out for that bill," Edwin said. There was a menacing hook on the end of the black bill. "It could tear your hands to

A jackass penguin by the entrance to its underground burrow

ribbons." Mr. Booth stepped aside, and the bird resumed plodding uphill.

Jackass penguins do not nest in colonies but dig burrows in the soft peaty soil. We found several of them, and in one saw an incubating bird far back in the shadows. These penguins start laying early, and there were already eggs in the burrows—safe from all predators, except a man with the long hooked wire that is used for "egging" jackass penguins.

We were about to start back to Sparrow Cove when Sewall, scanning the beach with his field glasses shouted, "Edwin, look! Over there. Is it a sheathbill?" He ran toward the beach, then slowed and advanced cautiously toward a bird, that looked exactly like a pure white pigeon, feeding on the beach. Sewall's stealthy approach caused a slight disturbance among the jackass penguins and logger ducks, and the bird looked up and saw its first ornithologist. It paused only a moment then walked straight toward him. They stood staring at each other ten feet apart. Then, bored, the sheathbill returned to its feeding, and the ornithologist climbed back up the hill.

"I can't believe it," he exclaimed. "That bird wasn't a bit afraid. What do you do, put salt on their tails?"

"Regularly," said Edwin, solemnly.

Sewall was excited because the sheathbill, the world's southernmost bird without webbed feet, nests in Antarctica and is only a visitor in the Falklands. Seeing one there was unexpected luck. The sheathbill has a growth of tissue above its bill, and is known to sailors by the uncomplimentary name of snotty nose.

We returned to Sparrow Cove over the shoulder of Mount Lowe. The higher we climbed the rougher the terrain became and the sparser the vegetation between the rock outcrops. Instead of white grass and diddle-dee we saw bright green mounds, almost six feet in diameter, that looked like moss-covered rocks. When you stepped on one, you sank disconcertingly into a soft mass. Mr. Booth called them balsam bogs and tore one apart to show us that it was composed of many tiny plants tightly packed together. If a piece was removed, the moisture would seep in and the whole bog would rot.

Heavy clouds moved in as we crossed the flank of the mountain and the rain and sleet were so blinding that we could not even see the outline of the hull of the *Great Britain*. We crouched miserably on the shore waiting for the *Stockfish*. By the time it came my left leg was so stiff that I had to lift it with both hands to get it over the side of the boat. When we reached home, I was too tired even to be impressed by the engraved invitation to dinner at Government House—Tuesday night, black tie, reply to aide-de-camp. By that time I would be dead and glad of it.

Surprisingly, the next morning I awoke in perfect health without an ache or pain, walked six miles over Sappers Hill to Mullet Creek without a complaint and had strength enough left to make out a list of the supplies we would need on Wednesday for our stay on Charles Point.

Sewall had found a man with a Land-Rover to taxi us and our equipment in and around Stanley. There were only about two hundred cars in the town, and only two Land-Rovers. Actually there was no place to go except six miles east to the lighthouse on Pembroke Point, or three miles west into the foothills of the Twin Sisters, two mountains at the head of Stanley Harbour. The roads, where they existed at all, were incredibly bad; but anyway we were glad to find a means of transporting our heavy cameras and tripods from the Cawkells' house to the jetty.

Sewall was determined to use the Land-Rover regardless of weather, and so we tried an expedition. It was the roughest ride I have ever taken, and I was afraid not only for our very bones but for the cameras and lenses we had protected so carefully. In time I learned to relax in a Land-Rover and ride the bumps, but on the first trip I was tense.

The driver, Tommy Goodwin, a bright, cheery man, drove us east to within two miles of a beach where gentoo penguins were supposed to spend their afternoons.

"Just walk that way," he said with a vague, careless wave of his hand. "You can't miss the pen-wings."

We found them all right, but the trip was not a success. Two yards, let alone two miles, was too far to carry all the equipment Sewall had insisted on bringing. The lack of carrying power was to plague us repeatedly for months to come. The wind, when it wasn't bringing rain or sleet, lifted the fine beach sand and drove it against us so furiously that we did not dare open a camera to change a film. And there was no activity among the penguins on the beach, nothing to photograph. It was their rest hour and they slept, some standing erect with heads under flippers, others prone, half-buried in the sand. When I got home I was too sanded, wind-blasted, and bone tired to think of the dinner at Government House that we were to attend that night.

It took real stamina to bathe and dress for that dinner. I tried to believe that Edwin was right when he said there was no need for heat in the bathroom—the tub of water would warm even this large room with its walls of a sickly color that Mary Cawkell called "government green." I forgot the cold when I saw the water. I knew it would be tinged with brown from having been leached from peat bogs, but I was unprepared for what looked like strong tea. If milk baths are good, maybe tea is better, I thought; and it was a good bath, although it was disconcerting not to be able to see my feet in the water.

Sewall's dinner jacket, which I had pressed myself because there was no tailor in Stanley, looked as if it had been washed in by the tide. The low-necked, sleeveless wisp of nylon that was my dinner dress appalled me. I knew I would freeze.

"Maybe I could wear this?" I asked Mary hopefully, pointing to a long-sleeved afternoon dress of soft wool.

"Oh, no," she said firmly.

"You won't freeze," Edwin called from the next room, "you'll suffocate. Central heating. It'll be even worse tonight because the Governor has a cold."

A car drew up in front of the house at five minutes before eight. As we were leaving, I looked at Sewall with envy. The orlon woolies showed only occasionally from under his stiff cuffs. Lucky males! As he let us out the door, Edwin admonished us to leave the party at ten minutes past ten—exactly.

In the car were Dr. and Mrs. Stuart Slessor. He was chief medical officer in the colony, and they were to be the only two other guests at Government House that evening. When we arrived, a footman and two maids were waiting at the door, and Mrs. Slessor and I were led quickly to an upstairs room. We put our ruffled hair in place and descended the stairs at the foot of which the men waited. I noticed an amused expression on Sewall's face. Beside him stood Dr. Slessor in the formal attire of a true Scot— black tie, black jacket with silver buttons, and kilts, below which his red knees peeked. I marveled; what kind of man was this who would choose to be so exposed when he could wear trousers and long underwear?

We were ushered into a long drawing room, at the far end of which Sir Miles and Lady Clifford waited before a blazing fire. Sherry was served at once, and almost before we had a chance to look around at the enormous bouquets of roses and snapdragons, dinner was announced. We were led single-file, double-time, down long, frigid passages, past portraits of British monarchs to a dining room, where we were speedily seated at a vast mahogany table. At each place was a dazzling array of crystal, silver, and linen.

Because of his cold, the Governor, sneezing, red-nosed, and watery-eyed, was anxious to have the whole thing over. Strict formality, however, was observed through all the courses. The distance that separated the guests was so great that we had to speak loudly and distinctly. While the table was being cleared of everything, including the place mats, I made the mistake of beginning a long and involved story. I was approaching the climax when a decanter and six glasses were placed before the Governor. He filled them and they were passed to us. Desperately, I tried to reach my punch line. When I paused to catch my breath, the Governor was on his feet.

"To the Queen!" he cried hoarsely, lifting his glass. Sewall had been well ahead of me. I settled back, hoping to be asked to finish my story, but the Governor was on his feet again.

"To the President of the United States!" he fairly shouted.

Looking across the expanse of mahogany I saw that Sewall was having difficulty. He had relaxed and wound his legs around his chair, and finished his wine. "Ike wouldn't have been proud of me," he said later. "I had to drink his toast with an empty glass."

Following these ceremonies, the table was reset and the last course of fruit and nuts was served. Then the ladies retired to the drawing room, where we chatted easily. Lady Clifford had been in the Falklands only since May and expected to leave in January when the Governor retired. I asked about the flowers and she told me they had all been raised in the conservatory of Government House. She asked me about penguins. When their young hatched would we accompany her to the penguin colony? She thought she ought to see one before she left. She was asking us for a guided tour, and we'd been in the Falklands only five days.

By the time the men joined us for coffee and liqueur, the Governor looked utterly miserable, but nobody made a move to break up the party. The moment for departure had not yet arrived. I watched the clock. Just as the hands reached ten after ten, Dr. Slessor jumped up in the middle of a sentence. We said good night and swiftly left the room.

As we walked out of the warm room, I wondered what Sir Ernest Shackleton had complained about? After all, when he was in the Falklands, he lived at Government House.

Gentoos celebrate reunion with their mates by trumpeting

Chapter 3

CHARLES POINT

The weather was miserable Wednesday morning, but Mary Cawkell decided to go with us just for the ride. She hadn't been out of Stanley in months, and never to Charles Point.

We stood on the jetty watching the ugly, lead-colored *Stockfish* approach over the rough water.

"Why does everything have to be so drab?" I asked. "Why don't they paint that boat a bright color and give the boatman a gay jacket?"

"It's always this way," Mary said.

"Don't the hills ever turn just a little bit green in the summer?"

"Never. Everything is gray and brown around Stanley. The people dress the same way. There's nothing bright in the shops." Mary, a trim figure in a vivid green coat, stood out against the drabness around her.

The *Stockfish* drew alongside and we climbed aboard. The sea was running high, but we chose to stand in the open cockpit and risk being soaked by the spray rather than crawl into the dark, airless hold. Down the harbor we passed close to a warship. I pointed and shouted over the roar of the wind: "Visitors?" "Frigate," Mary yelled back. "She's based here. Keeps the Argentines away."

Half an hour later we dropped anchor in Rabbit Cove. A dozen gentoo penguins eyed us as we rowed ashore in the dory and, burdened with food and cameras, climbed up the steep hill to the hut. I ushered Mary through the sagging door.

"You're going to be awfully cold," she observed cheerfully. "Why don't you build a fire there?" She pointed to a round cement block set in the floor, and inspected several holes in the roof.

"Fill the place with smoke," Sewall said grimly, "but we might try it."

Three small windows like portholes faced north and east across Port William. The single door opened toward Mount Lowe.

"Anyway, there are no ants to get in your food, no flies or mosquitoes," Mary said.

"And no snakes to crawl in the sleeping bag," Sewall said. "Just wind." A blast rocked the hut.

"I'm glad it's anchored down with all this sod," Mary said.

"This hut's been here ten years," the boatman said. "Was an outlook during the war." He was fidgety, anxious to be away before the weather got worse.

"We'll be back Sunday," Mary called, and I gloomily watched her go down the hill after the boatman. If we have to, I told myself, we could always walk back home. I could see Stanley. But distances were deceptive in the Falklands; it was a good twenty-mile hike around the harbors.

We watched the *Stockfish* out of sight, then stowed away the duffle and set off to Arrow Point and the gentoo penguin colony, just visible about a mile away. A great change had taken place since our visit the previous Saturday. Incubation was well under way; most of the penguins were sitting on nests barely three feet apart. A few birds stood beside their incubating spouses, flippers at their sides, their heads drooping.

I felt a wave of disappointment. In all the pictures I had seen of penguins, the birds were staring at people. Here were hundreds of birds paying no attention to us, not even bothering to look in our direction. It was deflating to the ego.

After we had watched them awhile we realized that there was a lot of quiet activity. Many birds were attending to their own nests, but a few were busy filching diddle-dee twigs from their neighbors'. There were acres of diddle-dee just at hand, but the twigs from the nests of their neighbors were, apparently, more desirable. Rather than venture out of the colony, a penguin would risk blows from beaks and flippers for the sake of a second-hand twig.

If a pair left a nest unguarded, it was stripped in no time, and all that was left was a bare depression containing two eggs. Some thieves did not even wait for a nest to be left unguarded but surreptitiously lifted twigs from nests while the occupants were snoozing. This seemed to require high talent, better developed in some individuals than in others. If a penguin got caught, he received blows from the owners' flippers and fearful thrusts from their sharp beaks. When birds returned to their nests with their loot, they laid each twig gently on the ground beside the incubating mate. One bird came toward us with a big twig. It stepped too close to another's nest and was poked from behind. It jumped aside, tramped another nest, and was pinched in the ribs. When it reached an open space it just stood looking around.

"That bird's lost, I swear it is," Sewall said.

The penguin turned around, walked back, and deposited the twig beside its nest. Looking over the rows and rows of incubating birds, I wondered how a penguin could find its own nest. Perhaps it was his mate he recognized; there was nearly always a bird on every nest.

*Gentoos steal diddle-dee twigs from each
other to build their nests*

We decided to go back to the hut for the cameras and start photographing. Dark clouds gathered ominously over Mount Lowe and the light was poor for photography, but we carried the cameras and tripod back to the gentoo colony and set them up. In every other bird colony where we had worked, it had been necessary for Sewall to photograph from a blind, while I walked away to make the birds, which were unable to count to two, think that we had both left. Here no blind was necessary or possible; I could not believe the penguins were so tame.

Sewall began photographing, and I returned to the hut and checked over the supplies I had bought in Stanley the day before. The Falkland Islands Company store had limited stocks—none of the campers' stand-bys such as pork and beans, corned beef hash, or Spam. After I had learned that canned meat was called tinned meat, crackers biscuits, mayonnaise salad cream, and candy sweets, I had managed to buy some Danish ham, tinned sausages, soup, vegetables, bacon, butter, and cheese. I'd had a hard time getting a tin for the paraffin, and realized that in Stanley one could not go anywhere else for what was unavailable. One took what was in the shops or waited for the *Fitzroy* to bring a new supply.

I decided shortly that the world outside was better than the chilly interior of the hut. I found the well, and following Stuart Booth's directions, dipped out the algae. That took all of fifteen minutes; the whole afternoon stretched ahead. I decided to take the new Leica mounted on a gunstock and photograph the rock shags we had seen off the point.

With the wind at my back I walked downhill along a narrow ridge to the very tip of Charles Point, and stood on a cliff about twenty feet above the sea. Just off the point a high triangular rock emerged from the water. On the almost sheer wall that faced me dozens of cormorant-like birds were leisurely constructing nests on narrow projecting shelves.

The rock shags were far more colorful than their cousins who inhabit the northeastern coast of the United States. Their backs, heads, and wings were glistening, almost purple black; their bellies were white; they had white patches on their cheeks, reddish chins, bright red eyes, and huge flesh-colored feet.

I found shelter behind a boulder and unpacked the camera.

Through the telephoto lens the birds were vivid. Several flew to the nesting rock, coming in low over the water, necks extended and mouths loaded with pink sea moss. They swooped up to land beside their mates, which were fashioning the nests. It was a bizarre courtship ritual: each male on arriving ceremoniously presented the sea moss to his mate. She accepted it and added it to the sloppy pile around her. The pair then swayed back and forth with heads stretched as high as their snakelike necks would permit, and nibbled each other around the face and throat.

I was so absorbed in trying to adjust the camera to the ever changing light and watching the curious mating antics of the birds that I forgot about the weather until a sudden fierce blast on my back made me look around. Mount Lowe had disappeared, the hut had vanished, the whole of Charles Point was blurred by whirling snow. <ins>1140597</ins>

Shoving the camera into its box, I jumped up and started to run uphill against the wind along the ridge toward the hut. A driving wind caught the cumbersome box broadside and nearly tore it from my hand. I fell, got up, wrapped my arms around the box, stumbled, and fell again. With sleet stinging my face, I covered the last few feet to the hut, crawling and dragging the camera. I slammed the door behind me and cowered in a corner while rain and hail pounded like fury on the tin roof.

I caught my breath and wondered if Sewall had been blown into the sea. He could cover the cameras, but he himself would be soaked and freezing. I focused the binoculars through the porthole. At last, as the storm moved on, I spotted a tan hump amid the black and white birds of the penguin colony. Slipping my new fisherman's raincoat over my head and carrying Sewall's, I set out on the run to the rescue. The lounging penguins fled as I hurried across the beach. By the time I had climbed the bluff and reached the edge of the colony, the sun was out and a cold wind was drying everything in its wake—everything but me. I was steaming in a rubber shell. Sewall was so intent on his pictures that he never looked up.

Feeling silly after such panic, I turned back without even calling to him. I took off the raincoat—I never wore it again—and flung myself down on a bank high above the beach to rest and to watch the penguins below.

Gentoos on the beach at Rabbit Cove

It was soon apparent that not all the birds on the beach were loafers. A few of them had been asleep there for hours; but for the most part Rabbit Cove was not a club for the idle but a landing place for the birds that nested on the bluff. Now, in the afternoon, they were arriving in small groups. I watched them far out in the harbor, porpoising toward the beach and hurling themselves out of the water like so many blunt-nosed bullets. If they arrived between breakers, black streaks shot under the shallow water and, like magic, penguins appeared. If their approach coincided with a wave, almost anything could happen. Often, misjudging the depth, they landed on their bellies, stumbled, and fell; sometimes they returned to the water and landed over again, as if to regain poise. I never heard them make much noise except for occasional short calls. Some went pattering up the beach to join the crowd immediately; others stood stock still and tucked heads under flippers, as though embarrassed at finding themselves there. A few paused at the edge of the water in an attitude of surprise and bewilderment, as though trying to figure out why they had come. Eventually they all edged up the beach and became part of the group.

After four-thirty, they landed in greater numbers, but the number on the beach remained almost constant—about twenty-eight or thirty birds. With all the room on the beach, the landing area appeared to have definite boundaries: it seemed to be only about twenty feet wide. Penguins that landed outside the strip either returned to the sea to try again, or raced pell mell, often using their flippers as forefeet, across the sand to join the gang. A gentoo penguin was never happy alone; neither was it happy too close to another.

The birds seemed to be moved by pressure from behind. When the landing area became too crowded, several of them broke away, climbed the bank, and started single file overland to the colony. Once started up the homeward trail, they were loath to turn back, although there were many pauses and delays. A resting group was usually reactivated by a penguin in the rear, charging into the lead with a "Let's get on with it, boys." When several birds became startled and hesitated, a penguin trudging behind, unaware of the alarm, continued forward unconcernedly. This detached attitude seemed to reassure them and they continued their journey. They had to keep moving to make room for new arrivals.

The path, the same from day to day, stood out against the gray sheep pasture. Even now in the early spring it was faintly green. The farmers liked gentoo penguins, for the grass grew best in their deserted colonies and along their paths. The length of this path—up a small valley, over a ridge, and through a peat bog—must have been nearly a mile. To follow it took some time, perhaps an hour or more, with frequent stops along the way. There was a brook to cross and some banks to climb, both requiring careful footwork. The colony was just above the landing place and could have been reached in five minutes; the long walk seemed ridiculous.

As it grew later, the distance between groups on the path diminished until at last there was a solid parade of penguins from beach to colony. Occasionally a penguin shot out of the water, hustled up the beach through a throng of loafers, and looking neither to right or left started up the path, like a person behind schedule muttering to himself, "Am I ever going to catch it for being so late!" One or two others sometimes eyed the worried bird casually, as if to say "What's all the rush?" A few loafers, seeing a hurrying penguin, joined it as though they had suddenly remembered that they too had obligations.

When I went back to help Sewall carry the cameras to the hut, I tried to tell him about the penguins on the beach; but he was too excited about the penguins in the colony to listen. While I cooked dinner in relays on the one-burner stove, he talked of their pilfering, quarreling, and trumpeting.

The author standing by a tussock bog on Kidney Island

"About four o'clock," he told me, "they began to come into the colony in increasing numbers. There must be twice as many birds there at night.

"Sometimes they get lost when they go home. The penguins that nest in the middle of the colony have a frightful time. They run between rows of nests and all the other penguins make passes at them. Sometimes they get so confused they run right through the colony and have to start over again. When they finally arrive at home base they stretch their necks straight up and trumpet. Did you notice how much noisier it was this evening than this afternoon?"

I said I had noticed nothing but the wind. I asked him about the squall. "Oh, that," he said. "It did take me by surprise, but I covered the camera and sat down on the ground and hung onto the tripod. I decided if it went into Port William, so would I. Where were you?"

"Just down on the point photographing rock shags," I said casually.

The weather turned from bad to worse and the squalls became more frequent; the temperature in the hut ranged from the 40's by day to the 30's by night. The sleeping bags were adequate, but leaving them in the morning was sheer torture. Cooking breakfast in relays on the primus and having bacon, eggs, and toast congeal almost before they left the stove was frustrating. We burned our lips on the first swallow of coffee from aluminum cups and complained moments later that it was stone cold.

Sewall brought home a penguin egg one night and asked to have it for breakfast. I cooked it carefully; to my annoyance the white would not become opaque; it remained like so much glassy jelly. I watched Sewall taste it. "Wonderful," he said, "break down and try some." I refused. He finished the egg but, strangely, never brought home another.

Each evening we tried with cramped icy fingers to record the events of the day. "Field notes should *never* be neglected," Sewall insisted. Sometimes we hung our coats over the door to keep out the drafts; sometimes we put them on and endured the breezes. When the primus was burning, they had to be hung over the door.

After two days Sewall announced that he could stand the cold no longer. He was going to build a stove. Scattered about the hut were the remnants of army occupation: dugouts, gun emplacements, braces for searchlights, cartridge boxes, old oil drums, odd bits of metal, wood, and peat. We used the cartridge boxes for tables, chairs, and storage from the first. Now, with a cut-down oil drum, a sheet of metal, lengths of stovepipe, fragments of wire, and Yankee ingenuity, Sewall constructed a stove on the cement block, with the pipe leading out of a hole in the roof. Cautiously he lit a few diddle-dee twigs. Smoke rose from the drum and went out the pipe. It worked until we tried to burn bits of wood over five inches long. Then smoke filled the hut. Nevertheless, the presence of flame and the sound of crackling wood were a comfort even with smoke in our eyes.

As a place to live, Charles Point was a failure; but from the ornithologist's point of view, it was a great success. Sewall spent most of the daylight hours in the gentoo colony, while I explored the coast of Port William, walking fast to keep warm. I discovered another gentoo colony in a nearby cove—a small, solid circle of nests in a level, grassy area quite close to a beach. But the birds in this colony were easily disturbed and fled to the water when I approached. Perhaps being fewer in number they did not feel as secure as the penguins in the larger colony. In the afternoon about four-thirty I wandered back to the bank above Rabbit Cove beach to watch the penguins come porpoising in from the sea. Sewall joined me, after working in the colony all afternoon.

"This porpoising and landing is the first job we'll tackle when we come back," he said.

I stared at him. How could he speak of coming *back* to this dreary, barren sheep pasture.

Saturday morning was frightful. Strong winds whipped the snow; and there was no point in trying to go to the colony. The snow never accumulated; wind blew it along the ground and it kept going. About midmorning I saw a ship enter Port William, the only craft we had seen in four days. Vanishing and reappearing in the snow squalls, she moved swiftly to the Narrows. There she circled, stopped, and circled again. I thought she was out of control and watched to see a shipwreck. But she passed through the Narrows and out of sight.

Later I learned that she was the *John Biscoe,* supply ship for

South Georgia and the Falkland Islands Dependencies, straight from England on her first voyage of the season. She had radioed her arrival time as eleven, and was stalling in Port William so that she could dock on the minute and be met by the Governor with ceremony. Apparently the radio operator failed to inform the captain that Sir Miles Clifford was in bed with a cold. Few citizens even saw the *John Biscoe* arrive, and no one ventured to the jetty to spread a red carpet.

I was glad to see Edwin and the *Stockfish* on Sunday. He said he had almost come to get us after the storm the day before, but Mary had persuaded him not to—we would either be dead or out photographing; so he had ridden on horseback to the far side of Port William and was relieved to see, through his field glasses, that Sewall was at work in the colony.

When we got to the Cawkells' the house seemed warm for the first time. I started to complain to Mary about the discomforts of Charles Point but instead found myself talking enthusiastically about the antics of the gentoo penguins.

Rockhopper penguins at their nest

Chapter 4

KIDNEY ISLAND

"You'll live comfortably on Kidney Island," Edwin said, after I had described some of the inconveniences of Charles Point. "It's a good hut, with a good stove. Plenty of birds, and sea lions too. They sleep in the tussock grass."

But when the day came for us to leave, Edwin was distraught. The *Philomel,* the government ship he had engaged to take us, was not in Stanley and might not be in for a week. The *Stockfish* was not insured to leave the harbor, and even if we could get permission, he doubted that it could make the short trip over the rough water off Mengeary Point. The only other possibility was the *Protector,* a cargo vessel now loading to go around the camp. The captain was willing to take us to Kidney Island—for a price: seventy dollars.

I winced. But Sewall said we'd take it.

I went shopping for supplies, including one hundred pounds of coal for the stove. When I ordered it, I knew why everyone burned peat. Coal was ninety dollars a ton.

Then I went to the spic and span Kelper store to engage Tommy Goodwin and the Land-Rover to take us to the jetty. A pleasant woman stood behind a counter of rings and bracelets set with Falkland Island pebbles—very hard agates—and I made a note to buy some. "Tommy Goodwin is in the next building working with the minerals," the woman said. I hadn't known that it was Tommy who set these stones in silver.

I went next door to find him. He was busy filling bottles with soda pop from large tanks. Minerals? Agates? Mineral water, of course.

Mr. Goodwin was delighted to be asked to drive us to the jetty at four—and would we mind if he came along on the trip?

"Of course not," I said. "It's a big ship. Bring someone else too if you like."

On the way back, I met Mr. Rowe, the banker, who asked me what arrangements we had made for emergencies. When I said none, he advised us to take a walkie-talkie so we could report to Stanley once a day. But we already had too much gear; and Edwin said that when he went to Kidney Island he always phoned the lighthouse keeper and told him he was going and would build a fire if he got in trouble. We could do the same.

"Everybody knows you're going," he added. "Some of them will be at the jetty to see you off."

"And some are coming with us," I told him.

He glowered. "None of them is going ashore. If they think they're going out there to collect penguin eggs, they're just dead wrong."

I felt like Mrs. Astor when I walked up the gangplank of the *Protector,* Mrs. Astor boarding her yacht in blue jeans, Mrs. Astor greeting her guests and hovering over a bag of coal more precious than gold. Mr. Goodwin was there with several strange gentlemen. Rowan came right from school, and there were other youngsters, children of the crew and friends. Mary, Edwin, Sewall, and I had tea in the tiny saloon. It was all quite jolly, like a holiday outing, and after we passed Mengeary Point, quite rough. Of course there was no sun. We hadn't seen the sun for more than five minutes at a time since we arrived, and by the time we dropped anchor in the kelp-enclosed harbor of Kidney Island it was raining.

There was a path up the steep thirty-foot rise to the hut, but we couldn't find it. With the crew of the ship hauling the supplies and equipment, we forced our way through dense grass higher than our heads, pulling ourselves up by grasping the blades, then sliding back on the wet slippery ground. Finally we emerged on a level open area and hurried toward the hut.

Edwin looked in and stood speechless. I looked in, and felt nausea coming on. This was the hut where we were going to live so comfortably. There were broken bottles, smashed dishes, overturned lamps, scattered playing cards, torn clothing, greasy pans, and everywhere the unmistakable signs of birds—big birds. Newspapers were ripped to shreds, bits of linoleum chewed up, a nest started here, a pile of ashes there, hunks of coal every-where.

"Someone left the door open," Mary said weakly.

Edwin looked so stricken that I felt sorry for him.

At that moment, several sharp toots came from the *Protector*. Her captain, like all captains in the Falklands, felt a storm coming. The crew put down their load. They must go. The Cawkells must go. In a matter of seconds we were alone on Kidney Island.

I didn't think we could do it, but we did. Starting at the stove in the far end of the hut, we pushed north through the door—shoveled, swept, and finally scrubbed. Everything in the hut was either washed or tossed into the tussock. The odor of birds remained—it probably always will—but otherwise the hut was as clean as human hands and cold water could make it.

The hut had been built by the government to house the tussock cutters who came yearly, if small boats were available, to harvest tussock grass for the Stanley cattle. It had built-in bunks, tables, benches, and shelves to make housekeeping convenient, and a real stove to warm it. From the wreckage we salvaged dishes, pans, a ship's teakettle, and even a scrap of carpet—all donations, no doubt, of previous occupants. Now it was in order. At ten-thirty we sat down to dinner cooked over a coal fire in the stove, then with the last of our strength blew up our rubber mattresses and crawled into our sleeping bags.

We were awakened at dawn by something big landing smack on the tin roof, then scratching and clawing its way to the ridge pole.

"Bird," Sewall said, and was out the door with me after him. A turkey vulture sailed off into the wind, then returned with three more, circling over us hopefully again and again.

At breakfast we studied a map that Edwin had drawn of the small island. Directly north of the hut the land rose to a high ridge running east and west to form a sort of backbone of the island. Beyond that the terrain dipped down abruptly and leveled off to the edge of the cliffs where the rockhopper penguins lived. It did not seem far from the hut, up over the ridge and down to the penguin colony—or so we thought until we learned about tussock bogs.

The early settlers in the Falklands found tussock grass covering all the small islands and ringing the larger ones. In order to grow, they said, tussock grass must "feel" salt spray on its blades. Their livestock, emaciated after the long voyage from England, grew fat on tussock, but wherever sheep were pastured, tussock disappeared. Now tussock is limited to the smaller islands and headlands from which sheep have been barred. Kidney Island was completely covered by it; because of the shortage of boats, it had not been cut for two years.

A gentoo trumpeting

We set out for the northern cliffs. Only a short distance from the hut we found ourselves enveloped in tussock. Numberless tussock plants with waving blades five or six feet long sprouted from pedestals composed of the tough entwined roots and stems of former plants. A single pedestal, often as high as my head, together with its fountain of green, is called a tussock bog. Where the old blades were broken off, I could walk between the chunky, irregular bases beneath a canopy of green; but more often the canopy was just at eye level, and I could not walk under it or see over it.

The bogs were just far enough apart to prevent our hopping from one to another, but close enough for their blades to entwine to form an impenetrable wall. Along with the physical exertion required to make our way in the tussock I had an intense feeling of claustrophobia that came over me in waves as we pushed, climbed, crawled, or stumbled, getting nowhere. Sewall, six inches taller than I, fared better, and went ahead to break the path. After we crossed the ridge the ground became wetter and before we reached the cliffs we were wallowing in a filthy morass.

We smelled and heard the rockhopper penguins long before we saw them. I had sniffed at the slight odor from the gentoo colony, which was washed clean by constant showers and dried by brisk winds; but I nearly gagged at the stench that rose from the rockhoppers' premises, damp, shaded, and surrounded by tussock. Old tussock bogs served as nest sites; dried blades of grass were heaped around dirty eggs. Little creatures with mud-stained plumage peered at us around every bog and vigorously protested our passage through their colony.

I was so intent on trying to find a solid place to put my foot that I did not notice an angry little penguin that shot like a fox terrier from behind a tussock bog, latched onto my leg just above my high boot, and beat me viciously with its flippers. I screamed, kicked, and stamped to shake it off, and clawed at the tussock bog to keep from falling into the mire. The bird fled as Sewall crashed back through the tussock.

I looked from my bleeding leg to his laughing face. "It hurt!" I cried angrily.

"Stop groaning," he said, "after all there aren't many women in the world lucky enough to be bitten by a penguin."

After that I carried a stick to ward off attacking penguins, but none ever came near me again, and although they made a lot of noise, most of them paid no more attention to us than the gentoos had.

A rockhopper sitting on its eggs

On the cliffs we had our first good look at rockhopper penguins. Here clean little birds guarded eggs or worked on nests of pebbles and tussock grass in crevices all up and down the steep rocks, a precarious location for a colony of flightless birds. They were small, about half the size of gentoos, and their distinguishing feature, a streak of yellow feathers that slanted upward above each red eye and formed a tuft above each ear, gave them an oriental look. When they were disturbed the black feathers on their heads stood straight up, turning them into fierce little monsters. The din was terrific. At first we thought that our invading their cliffs was the cause; later we discovered that rockhoppers are just plain noisy all the time.

To avoid the tussock, we returned to the hut along the shore, circling the eastern end of the island. As Edwin had said, it was an ornithologist's dream. The rockhopper penguin colony blended into the colony of king shags. They waggled their heads at us but never left their enormous nests of tussock and seaweed that dotted the face of the cliff.

King shags

King shags, also called blue-eyed shags, are extraordinary creatures with black backs, white fronts, orange caruncles at the base of the bill and several curly black plumes on the top of the head. Their brown eyes are circled by a band of vivid violet-blue skin.

At the eastern end of the island where the cliffs broke down into a boulder beach, we found a pair of black oystercatchers. They were the same size and shape as the black and white variety but they were totally black except for red bills and eyelids, yellow eyes, and pale beige feet and legs that looked nude, untanned, slightly unfinished. The birds screamed at us but did not fly from their beach. Sewall, studying the ecological niches of the oystercatchers, noted that the black ones inhabited boulder beaches, while the black and white ones were found on sand beaches.

We became aware of some small birds that followed our foot-steps across the kelp-strewn, rock beach. There were Falkland robins, wrens, and several dark birds, a little smaller than the robins but much bolder. Sewall identified the wren as Cobb's wren, a subspecies of the Neotropical house wren, found only in the Falklands. The brown bird was a tussockbird, belonging to the family of South American ovenbirds. One came right up to the toe of my boot and turned over bits of rotted kelp with quick flips of its bill. They were supposed to be so tame that they would light on a man's shoulder and tug at the hairs on the back of his neck.

But we forgot them when we saw, on the next promontory, a pure white goose, a large one, so striking against the dark water that I caught my breath. It was a kelp goose. It held its ground while we came close to see its black eyes, bill, and feet. We found its nest easily right on the edge of the tussock. An enormous bog leaned over it, the blades of grass forming a curtain that concealed the female. Black, barred with white, she sat calmly until we pushed her off the nest to count the eggs—seven—then slid back on.

Logger ducks yammered at us when we reached the sand beach where we had landed the previous day. I waved at them. This was ornithology as I liked it—not too many birds, all tame and easy to see, a far cry from chasing wood warblers in dense forests. This was fun. I was not yet aware of the thousands of petrels, fairy-like birds of the dusky twilight, that were at that very moment incubating thousands of eggs in thousands of burrows on Kidney Island.

As I charged down the beach I roused a sea lion from his nap on a bed of tussock. He rose up, puffed out his neck with its shaggy yellow mane, and gave out a terrific roar. At the same time he spouted steam, his breath condensing in the cold air. Then another roar, and another, as I froze in my tracks not six feet away.

I shrieked. "That's a dragon breathing fire!"

Sewall came up behind me laughing. "Don't go near him,"

He picked up a small rock and tossed it at the dragon. The beast slid from his bed and down along the worn rocks to the water. After sticking his head up and looking us over once more, he disappeared beneath the maze of kelp in the harbor.

"That, my pet, was a male sea lion," Sewall informed me. Male sea lions, or bulls, are dangerous only during the rutting season, September. This was October. They would not attack us. However, we must be careful not to be in the way when the huge, six hundred pound animals decided to take to the water.

From that moment on, the tussock, already unpleasant, held real terror. Every time I came to a place where the grass was matted down, I moved warily for fear of stepping on a sleeping sea lion.

All afternoon a storm raged across the island. The wind went down with the sun and night came on starlit and clear. Standing in the doorway of the hut we watched the beams of Pembroke Light sweep across the sky, and listened to the bellowing of the sea lions. It was cold, the air was crisp, but inside the hut it was warm and cozy.

The next morning we set out to make a trail through the tussock so that we could transport the cameras to the penguin cliffs. Hacking and chopping with a hatchet and saw (what they were doing on a treeless island I'll never know), we made our way to the top of the ridge, marking the trail with stakes cut from the ruins of an old shanty, and laying the freshly cut grass in the path.

When we advanced downhill into the filthy swamp, the rockhopper penguins were furious. They resented our approach as if we were a slum-clearance committee. We trimmed off the tops of bogs and sunlight poured into their odoriferous hollows. By lunchtime we had a trail we could follow, if we were careful.

A storm made photography impossible that afternoon. As I lay on my bunk listening to the sounds of the wind whipping the tussock against the tin walls of the hut and driving showers of rain in spasms on the roof, I fell asleep. Sometime during my nap Sewall took his Graflex and left the hut.

I slept on until the door burst open and Sewall said, "Hold everything, I've broken my arm!" I jumped to my feet. Sewall was leaning against the door jamb.

"That's all right," I heard myself saying, calmness struggling with utter confusion, "I'll splint it."

He sat down on a low bench and leaned on the upright that supported the bunks. His left arm hung limp. Slowly, inch by inch, I worked off his coat, and cut the sleeve from his sweater.

I was about to cut through his flannel shirt when I remembered
what I had learned in a wartime first-aid course: keep the patient
warm, no stimulants, watch for shock, above all, keep him warm.

It was cold in the hut and he was already shivering. If I cut
off the wool shirt and the underwear, how would I keep him
warm? And the fire—I had no idea how to run a coal stove.
He was frightfully pale.

"Let's look at the arm," I said, "then I'll splint it."

When I looked at it I forgot about splints: there was a huge
swelling around the shoulder. The break was very far up.

"It's the humerus, near the head," Sewall said. I let it go at
that. I was helpless. He was in great pain.

"Maybe I can fix a sling to take the pull off the shoulder?"
I suggested without conviction. The first-aid course had recommended substituting a pillow case for a proper sling. Where would
I find a pillow case on Kidney Island? I fashioned a sling from
a blouse and a scarf, wrapped the heavy coat around him, and
fastened it securely with a belt.

He was paler now and shivering even more. What to do for
shock? Whisky? No, not until all danger of shock had passed.
Coffee? Aspirin? Tea? Tea was safe enough. Waiting for the
water to boil on the primus, I poked at the stove, added coal,
and chatted endlessly—to myself. Sewall said not a word. Only
the desperation in his eyes told me what he was thinking. Here
we were, ready to go; all the time, energy, and thought—and
now this. Never in all our years together had life looked so
black.

With the hot, strong tea the color slowly returned to his lips
and the shivering lessened. He told me what had happened:
he was on a rocky ledge; he thought he'd get one more picture
of the kelp goose; then he slipped on a bit of spray-dampened
lichen. As he bent his arm to save a camera, all the weight
crashed down on his elbow. And now would I please just leave
him alone. Would I go for the camera on the ledge just opposite
the kelp goose's nest on the eastern end of the island.

"And while you're there," he added, "you might as well finish
off the film. It's probably ruined anyway." Then he said gently,
"I'm sorry I had to leave it. I tried. . . ."

"I don't mind," I said quickly. Suddenly I was anxious to
escape the hut and leave him alone. "I'm sorry I had to leave

it. . . ." If only he had yelled at me so that I could have yelled back and burst into tears.

Considering the steep bank of tussock and the high rocky ledges he had to climb over, it was a wonder he'd been able to get himself back, let alone the camera. The Graflex, sprayed by the surf, sat high on a rock in plain view. Although I'd had no intention of doing so, I couldn't resist using up the last four exposures on the black and white female kelp goose standing beside her nest, and the pure white male close by. But as I snapped the final picture, a huge wave—the seventh, I suppose— crashed against the ledge and drenched the camera and me.

"To hell with kelp geese," I screamed at the innocent birds, and started struggling back over the rocks.

Now I began to worry about getting help. The *Protector* would not call for us for a week. Somehow I must get in touch with Stanley. But how? I knew from our experience on Charles Point that I couldn't hope to hail a passing ship. I looked across the channel to Kidney Cove where we had lunched that first day. If only I were a good swimmer—but even if I could swim it, there would be too long a hike in icy clothes through snow and wind.

Edwin had mentioned lighting a fire, but the thought of it terrified me. A fire fanned by that driving wind would sweep across the whole island. No, that would only be a last resort. When I got back to the hut, I still had no solution.

Sewall had finished a second cup of tea. He managed a twisted smile when I showed him the water-soaked camera. "Looked bad enough before," he said, "but I don't think it'll be hurt if you take it apart and dry it right away."

This was a dangerous suggestion to make to anyone as unmechanical as I, but under his directions I took the camera apart and dried it carefully. Then I broached the subject of getting help.

"I think you can see the lighthouse from the top of the island," he said. "I'm quite sure I saw it this morning when I climbed one of the bogs to drive a stake."

"And . . .?"

"Simple. You can signal from there tonight with the big flashlight and the Stroboflash."

My hands went rigid. I nearly dropped the camera. I could not. I would not go into the tussock alone by day, let alone by night, for a broken arm, a camera, Walt Disney Productions, or anything else. I wouldn't.

All this I never said. Yes, I would. Just as soon as I finished drying the camera, I would go look for the lighthouse.

Even in daylight it was hard enough to follow the five stakes that marked the trail to the top of the ridge. I got lost several times before I reached the top and climbed on a bog higher than my head. I could see the lighthouse just over Mengeary Point. I shivered to think of coming back at night. I would need a wider path, much wider; a turnpike, in fact.

For the rest of the daylight hours I sawed tussock to widen the trail. As I cut, the blades left standing leaned over and twined together as if to compensate for their lost members and obscure the trail. At dusk I walked up and down again and again until I was sure I could follow the path with a flashlight. On one trip up I met a jackass penguin, the first I had seen on Kidney Island. Both surprised, we stopped and stared at each other. I kept my eyes on his vicious bill and waved my saw at him, saying "Shoo!" He stood his ground, wagged his head from side to side, and went on staring. I stepped aside and he waddled on by. After all, it was his path.

By this time Sewall was wretched with pain. The danger of shock seemed to have passed, so I gave him an iceless Scotch highball and looked in the carefully packed medicine kit for aspirin. The shock was mine. There were only four tablets left in the bottle. I concealed my chagrin at having neglected to check the kit, and gave him only one.

By the time we had eaten our gloomy dinner and I had learned to use the Stroboflash, a black night had closed over Kidney Island. Armed with the flashlight equipment and precious little courage, I started for the ridge. There was a strong, gusty wind; the sky was clear, the stars very far away and unfamiliar. The sounds of the surf crashing on the beach, the incessant clamor of rockhoppers on the cliffs, the roaring of the sea lions did not bother me; they were distant and identifiable. But there were sounds that were closer—moans and groans and cries from the tussock—that were frightening. Under my feet things scurried and rattled the dry grass. Something with big wings crossed the beam of the flashlight and was quickly gone. Looking back now, I do not see how I forced myself to climb that hill.

On the high bog, with the wind beating my back, I began to flash at regular intervals toward the lighthouse. Then I tried the Stroboflash, which went off with a brilliance that seemed to light up the entire island. After a few minutes my gloved hands were so numb with cold that I had to return to the hut.

"Any reply from the lighthouse?" Sewall asked.

"Of course not," I said scornfully. My grandfather had been a sea captain and had rounded the Horn any number of times in a sailing vessel. I was an authority on the sea. "They *never* change the rhythm of the light." I held my hands over the stove. "But Sewall, the noises in the tussock—they're horrible. It's crawling with groaning things. Sounds as though people were being murdered."

He tried to smile. "Probably just jackass penguins in their burrows, or maybe sooty shearwaters." I poked the stubborn fire in the stove. "The scurrying things in the path," he added, "may have been small gray-backed petrels, and the big flying birds were probably short-eared owls."

Every half hour until well after midnight I trudged to the ridge and flashed, but there was no response. Somehow I managed to help Sewall into his bunk, where he sat propped up with rubber mattresses, camera cases, and duffle bags. All through the long night I tended the fire and tried to read by the light of one candle. At dawn when Sewall seemed to be dozing, I fell onto my bunk still dressed. I had nearly gone to sleep when a turkey vulture arrived on the roof.

Disgusted, I got up and made coffee on the primus, and kicked angrily at the coal stove. The fire was completely dead. Then I went outside to scan the harbor for some sign of a ship.

About midmorning I nailed one of Sewall's whitest T shirts to a stick and set out for the signaling post. The path was broad and easy to follow by day; but now it was littered with dozens of soft, blue-gray wings—all that was left of the petrels killed during the night. My cutting the tussock had exposed their trails and burrows and made them easy prey for owls.

I tied the white flag to the stake on the highest bog with only a faint hope that it might be seen from a ship, a plane, or perhaps the lighthouse. If only the frigate would choose this clear, beautiful day for a reconnaissance of the coast, or the *John Biscoe* would leave for South Georgia.

As I ran downhill toward the hut I saw three turkey vultures, with wings spread, sunning themselves on the roof. This was too much. Breaking off chunks of tussock bog I rushed at them throwing wildly and screaming, "You get off this house!" They left in a huff and circled me sullenly. I was almost in tears. I had enough trouble without turkey vultures on the roof.

By afternoon I had more. Sewall had a fever. The wind rose steadily; the clouds closed in. It was colder than ever, 30° F., and I couldn't make the stove burn properly.

Long before dark I was on the signaling bog, ready to begin flashing as soon as the first beams appeared from Pembroke Light. Suddenly, while I waited, birds, big birds, circled silently over me, coming closer and closer until I shrunk from them. In a moment they were gone and the air seemed to fill with smaller birds whirling about. They too were gone quickly; and from the tussock came groans and cries.

Just then a beam of light passed over the island, and I flashed toward the lighthouse. Soon it seemed that the steady, rhythmic flashing of the light from across the water had changed. Was the pause between flashes longer than usual, or were my eyes playing tricks on me? I waited, but there were no more pauses.

I said nothing about the light when I went back to the hut; I did not want to raise false hopes in Sewall. But when I returned to the bog in fifteen minutes my first flash brought a definite reply. The light stopped turning and trained its beam straight on me. Before I was down off the bog, a searchlight cut the clouds in the direction of Stanley. The signal had been seen.

I ran to tell Sewall. "They can't come tonight," he said. "Not on a night like this." The wind was howling again.

I went to the ridge several more times and flashed, just in case. At ten-thirty I saw the lights of a ship off Mengeary Point.

Bursting into the hut, I cried, "They're coming," and started to pack. I gave Sewall the last two aspirin and a strong drink of whisky. Every movement caused him such pain I wondered how I would get him to the beach.

When I had finished packing I went out to check the progress of the ship. It had passed Kidney Island and was far out at sea.

I had to tell Sewall they weren't coming for us, but I knew they would be here in the morning. They had answered my signal.

The aspirin and whisky had eased Sewall's pain. "What were you flashing?" He asked.

"SOS," I said. "After all, I was a girl scout."

"My God! SOS means ship in distress. They don't even know it's you. They'll be out looking for a ship in trouble."

I looked at him in horror. What had I done? Sending false signals at sea was a serious crime; ignorance was no excuse. I saw myself court-martialed, put in irons. I could see the headlines: AMERICAN CITIZEN CONVICTED. POSSIBLE ESPIONAGE.

"They wouldn't expect a woman to know any signals," I said lamely.

"How do they know it's a woman?" Then he added, "Oh well, this is probably just a sprain anyway."

That did it. "Brother," I said icily, "this better be more than a sprain. If I've lured a ship out of a safe harbor on a night like this. . . ."

I tried to revive the dying fire. It was a relief to have something to poke. While Sewall dozed, I sat down and wrote the events of the past thirty-six hours in a letter to the children.

Shortly after one o'clock the wind slackened a bit and I could hear the crashing of the breakers. Suddenly a cry came out of the night: "Ahoy up there!"

I dashed outside into the blackness and followed the direction from which the voice had come off shore. Half rolling, half falling I got to the beach with my light and guided a dory in. A man jumped from the boat and said in a firm voice. "I'm John Huckle, Mrs. Pettingill. What's the matter?"

"Broken arm—pain—fever—cold," I stammered. Two more men appeared and drew the boat ashore.

"Do we need a stretcher?"

"I don't think so. Come and see."

We crawled up through the tussock. Sewall was already standing by the door, his leather case of field notes grasped in his good hand.

"We haven't a minute to lose because of the tide," John Huckle said. "Come at once. Leave everything right here."

"I can't go," I said flatly. "I can't leave the cameras here with this fire." I'd guarded the cameras too long; I'd stay alone on this horrible island rather than leave them now. "I won't go," I repeated.

"Mrs. Pettingill," he said. "You *will* go with your husband."
There was no compromise in his voice. Then he hesitated. "Mac
will stay. You'll stay, won't you, Mac? We'll be back for you
tomorrow."

Poor Mac, he had no choice. It was apparent that one did
not argue with Mr. Huckle.

Sewall passed me the leather case and went with the men.

I couldn't find my boots—the great high boots that I hated
yet had to have to get into the boat. While I hunted for them,
I tried to explain about the food supply to Mac who, instead of
listening, kept asking me for my "torch."

"Mac," I pleaded "Look for my boots. I can't get into that
boat in sneakers."

"Lady," he assured me solemnly, "I'll devote the rest of my
evening to it, if only you'll give me your torch." He pointed to
the flashlight in my hand. "Please leave it with me on the beach."

I gave up on the boots and we started for the beach. My
flashlight went out on the way down, but my calls for help went
unheeded. Sewall was seated in the stern of the dory when I fell
out of the tussock, passed the dead torch to Mac, and directed
by Mr. Huckle, waded into the icy water to sit in the stern beside
my husband.

"Somebody feed my little dog," Mac called as he pushed us off.

After several hair-raising false starts, we headed straight out
into the breakers and total darkness. The gale had subsided but
not the sea. I was on Sewall's left side, and couldn't put my
arm around him. I did not dare touch him so I took a firm grip
on the belt of his coat and held my breath. The stern of the
heavily loaded boat seemed barely four inches above the water.
So far there was no ship in sight.

The men rowed hard and finally we rounded a point and saw
the ship's lights.

The rollers at the point were so big that I expected each
wave to swamp the dory. Then we drew up on the leeward side of
the ship and bounced against her in the darkness. Flashing beams
came from the deck above.

The crew lowered a thick rope which John Huckle tied about
Sewall's waist, then a rope ladder. Supported from below by the
two men, Sewall stood on the ladder and held one side with his
good hand, while the crew on the deck pulled him up until they

could seize his right arm and lift him over the side. I was next. The rope ladder swung out with each roll of the ship and snapped back with a bang. Mr. Cawkell caught me as I struggled over the rail and almost fell on the deck.

In the captain's cabin Stuart Booth was trying to make Sewall comfortable, and the ship's cook appeared with mugs of hot tea.

Edwin was relieved that it was only a broken arm, and that our signal had not been seen on the previous night, for at that time there had been no ship to come for us. This ship—it was the *Philomel,* the government rescue ship—had returned at six this evening. Her crew had been discharged for an annual holiday —peat-cutting week. At eight-forty-five our signal was first seen by the lighthouse keeper. He acknowledged it by stopping the light for eight seconds, then telephoned John Huckle, the harbor-master in Stanley. At nine the six men of the crew of the *Philomel* were summoned by wireless—from bath, bar, and fireside. At nine-fifteen the ship was under way.

Because of the wild sea the captain had taken her far out before attempting to enter the narrow channel between Kidney Island and the mainland. They had been four hours on the way. Mr. Booth had been sick and Edwin hadn't had a quiet moment.

"About halfway out," Mr. Booth said. "Mr. Cawkell remembered your flash equipment and suggested—only suggested— that you might be taking night pictures of birds."

"And you should have heard the language of the crew," Edwin said, grinning. "It was—shocking."

When the dory had been raised and the *Philomel* was safely out of the channel, John Huckle joined us. "I thought that you two Americans were just out of paraffin for your primus. I was prepared to drown you on the spot." He assured me I had done no wrong in signaling, but, he added I was a failure as a girl scout.

"Not once did you send an SOS," he went on. "Better check up on the Morse code if you mean to do this often."

I tried to apologize for bringing them out in such weather; I had no way of telling them just how serious it was. I had not expected them to come at night. In fact I wished they had waited for daylight. It was wrong to risk lives.

John was consoling: "Don't worry about risking lives. They love it. They don't have excitement like this every day. It will provide conversation for weeks to come."

Sewall sat pale and silent in a corner. The effects of the mild sedative had worn off and the least movement made the pain almost intolerable. The ship crept slowly back to Stanley where we tied up at the jetty about three-thirty in the morning.

It was decided that Sewall should walk to the hospital rather than wait for Mr. Goodwin. "I couldn't stand the Land-Rover," he whispered to me. Edwin hurried ahead to alert the nurses.

"We'll not go back to Kidney Island this morning," John Huckle told me. "I'll give you a ring. Maybe Monday."

"And Mac?"

"He'll wait for us. By the way, you packed up all the liquor, didn't you?"

I knew I did. "In the camera cases," I told him. "What if he. . . .?"

"It's safe," he said. "He'll not open one thing, but . . . if it were in plain sight. . . ."

The three blocks to the hospital were probably the longest Sewall ever walked. The wind cut through our wet clothes; the stony road jogged the arm. He almost fell into the arms of the nurse who waited at the door.

When he was safely in bed, she vanished for a moment and returned with a loaded tea tray. Bless the British! Whatever the crisis, there is always time for a cup of tea. Dr. Slessor arrived and had his cup before confirming Sewall's diagnosis.

"Go home," he said to me, "and don't come back until I call you." He handed me a pill. "Take this and go to bed."

I was about to leave when I thought of something very important. "Will you try," I asked the doctor, "to get his underwear off without cutting it?"

He eyed me strangely. "What's so special about the underwear?"

I did not dare explain—not in this wool-producing colony. I was only sure that life would not be worth much without that orlon underwear. I smiled, said goodnight, and walked with Edwin into the wind. Great bunchy clouds in the east were turning pink and roosters were crowing all over town.

Cliffs at Kidney Island

Sewall Pettingill and "Pengy," a pet king penguin

Chapter 5

INTERLUDE

Sunday, November 8, was a lost day. I was only half awake when Dr. Slessor called on me. Sewall had a bad break near the head of the humerus; the arm would have to be in a cast for six weeks and it would be some time after that before he regained full use of it.

I was still stupefied by the powerful sleeping pill he had given me. As he left, he said, "I didn't cut the underwear—or the shirt."

I recall vaguely tottering to the hospital and entering the small white room. Sewall, perched high in bed and swathed in blankets, flung back the covers to show me an awesome triangular lump of plaster and steel where his arm should have been. I couldn't say anything and hid my face in a bouquet of yellow roses on the dresser. Then we sat and stared at each other. When the nurse brought tea, we drank it in silence. Sewall fell asleep and I crept out of the room and went home.

The Cawkells, about to leave for a cocktail party at Government House, told me we would go back to Kidney Island at eight the next morning; we should have gone today, Edwin said, it was fine weather. I suddenly realized that it was a beautiful day, the first we'd had. Mumbling regrets for Lady Clifford about the cocktail party, I went back to bed and slept until seven Monday morning.

The trip to Kidney Island was surprisingly easy this time. For a change, no one was in a hurry. John Huckle and the crew of six, well-rested and in high spirits, apparently bore me no ill will for their interrupted holiday. They speculated on whether Mac had found the whisky and how many penguin eggs he had collected—hundreds, they imagined. I knew better; there weren't that many to be had in the depleted colony of Kidney Island.

We dropped anchor off the island, and the cook served coffee and sandwiches before we went ashore in the small boat. The rope ladder was simple by day, and navigating the boat through the kelp was easy. I was not even annoyed at being soaked by the waves that broke over the side of the boat and the rain-laden tussock on the path to the hut.

Mac was standing steadily by the door, and I knew he had not found the whisky. When we left the shore with the last load of duffle I was quite relaxed. My boots, found in the coal hod, lay at my feet; in my lap I held a burlap bag containing a few penguin eggs. Mac was rather ashamed of his small harvest.

"It's all I had time to get," he said. "I had to stay by the hut and watch for you." He still would not admit that there weren't many eggs in the colony.

Edwin remarked later that he was relieved to know that the crew of the *Philomel* could not collect eggs because they had no licenses. I kept silent about Mac's meager collection.

The Falkland Islanders, like people everywhere, have abused their natural resources. The penguin colonies near settlements have dwindled alarmingly, and some have entirely disappeared. A few people like Edwin Cawkell have managed to curb the depradations; now a license is required for egging.

John Huckle had a different view. "The birds belong to the people," he had said that morning. "If the people want to destroy the birds, there'll be no more eggs, why all the fuss? It's everybody's hard luck."

"No," I argued. "The birds don't belong to these people. They belong to all people, including those to come. Wild living things don't belong to anybody."

It was midafternoon before I had our gear stowed away once more in the Cawkells' house and went to the hospital. Sewall was distraught; the doctor had forgotten him; the cast was unendurable; worst of all, he was out of tobacco. A nurse burst into the room.

"Now we must have our bath," she said cheerily.

I fled. Once outside, I suddenly realized that for the first time in months I had nothing to do but buy tobacco. The wheels had stopped. I began to share Sewall's black mood. But when I met strangers on the street who made kind inquiries about Sewall, I felt better. Heretofore we had been so absorbed in our job that we paid little attention to the Falkland Islanders, and they had coolly ignored us. Now the ice was melted. When I got back to the hospital the mood had changed. Several visitors had dropped in, the room was warm. After the wind, cold, and isolation of Kidney Island, the hospital was a haven of security. Although Sewall did not need me—the nurses gave him their undivided attention and guests kept popping in—I needed him, or more truthfully, his radiator. Often when no one was looking I sat on it to overcome my shivering.

Dr. Slessor brought us a very worn copy of *The Worst Journey in the World* by Apsley Cherry-Garrard, an account of the ill-fated Scott expedition. We rediscovered the pleasure of reading aloud; absorbed particularly by the chapter, "The Winter Journey," which describes the adventures of an ornithologist and two companions who ventured forth into the cold and darkness of the Antarctic night to collect the eggs of the emperor penguin, we completely forgot the broken arm and lost track of time.

In a few days Dr. Slessor, much to our relief, removed Sewall's cast and replaced it with a triangular basket of lightweight aluminum. He was now able to stand alone. I had to find a warm shirt that would fit over the cast. I looked for a wool one but found only rayon of poor quality.

"This is disgraceful," I told the clerk in the F.I.C. store. "No wool shirts in a wool-producing colony."

"But it's summer," he said, eyeing my storm coat critically. "I'll look in the attic."

He finally found one shirt, a sickly mustard yellow with a brown stripe, size 16½. Sewall wore size 15½. I had no compunction about ripping it to fit over the aluminum basket.

Sewall left the hospital after a week with great reluctance. He knew he was going to be cold, and he was. Edwin got him a Tilley heater for the bedroom, a balky contraption which, if primed often enough with methylated spirits, would burn paraffin. Mary and I were afraid of it, so was the maid, and Edwin didn't have time to fuss with it. Sewall spent most of each morning coaxing it to burn. When he first lighted it, flames spurted out followed by clouds of black smoke; then the mantle glowed, producing a steady roar. Sometimes he got the temperature in the room up to 65° by lunch time. I thought there was little to choose between pneumonia or carbon monoxide poisoning. But at least it kept him occupied.

We walked a bit each day. At first it was difficult; the wind caught Sewall's arm, which protruded like a wing, and twisted him sideways. We kept to the main road, visiting the policeman who doubled as the town barber, exploring the shops and buying sheaves of colorful Falkland stamps.

We had heard that the *Fitzroy* was loading for Montevideo and I wrote dozens of letters and decorated them with stamps until they looked like picture galleries: stamps with penguins, geese, swans, sheep, seals, and ships. Edwin shook his head. "They'll never reach the States," he said. "In the first place, it's illegal to post a letter with too many stamps. And even if they get by, they'll be stolen in Monte." He was right, of course; canceled Falkland Island stamps are valuable. Only a third of our letters ever reached their destinations.

Sewall could never stay long on a main road and soon we were venturing into the camp behind the house. Flowers were in bloom everywhere: among the mosses, pale maidens, white bell-shaped blossoms on slender, leafless stalks, braving the wind to a height of six or seven inches; between the rocks, pigberry plants with white flowers the size of strawberry blossoms. Oxalis grew in small clumps in dry sandy soil, with flowers, some pink and some white, and deeply serrated leaves. It is called scurvy grass because sailors coming ashore after a long voyage used to eat the leaves to prevent scurvy.

But we looked mainly for birds for me to photograph. In a gorse hedge we found a Falkland robin's nest with small young, and high on Sappers Hill a pipit's nest hidden in the thick grass. Edwin said they were very hard to find. I already knew that; after following Sewall for hours over the bleak, exposed flats, I hated pipits.

In Government Forest, a small plot of low, twisted evergreens behind Government House, we discovered a black-chinned siskin's nest with three eggs. The siskin, very like our American goldfinch but duller in hue, came boldly to the nest as we watched. When we told Edwin about it, he said we could not possibly have found a siskin; it nested only in West Falkland. He went to see for himself and returned somewhat annoyed. He liked things to be neatly catalogued and in their proper places; no self-respecting siskin had any right to nest in East Falkland—as everybody knew but the siskins.

When, two weeks after the accident, Dr. Slessor removed the aluminum basket from Sewall's arm and put it in a sling, with the warning that it might be half an inch shorter, we hardly heard him. We began to make plans for taking movies and the next day Mr. Goodwin drove us to the slaughterhouse in the Land-Rover.

So far all I had ever done with the movie cameras was carry them. Now after excitedly practicing changing films under a black hood, I set up the camera on the rim of a grassy bank about ten feet above the point where a huge iron pipe discharged offal into the harbor at intervals. The birds gathered about expectantly. Before I was quite ready, the pipe discharged and the water boiled as the birds rushed in—gulls from the air, stinkers from the water. I fumbled with the lens, grappled with the tripod as the camera swung wildly. I tried to focus everywhere, on the air full of beating wings, on the churning water. Before I had exposed twenty feet of film, Sewall pushed me aside and took over. By lowering the camera he was able to use both hands to operate it.

Feeling somewhat hurt, I picked up the Leica and went down to the beach. The sun came out, and I had time for one shot before I heard a cry for help and rushed back up the bank. A sudden squall had come; Sewall was desperately trying to protect the camera from the snow. I flung on the waterproof cover; we crouched on the ground beside it until the squall had passed, then Sewall resumed, while I watched the "peck order" among the birds. It was repeated over and over: each time the offal came out of the pipe, the screaming kelp gulls dived en masse from above; when they had grabbed their share, the stinkers dashed through the waves in wild confusion, playing tug of war with intestines and scrapping over brains as the water ran red with sheep's blood. After the kelp gulls and the stinkers had withdrawn, the dolphin gulls came in for the leavings. The large menacing skuas were not always around, but when they were they took precedence over all the others.

After the stinkers had gobbled up their loot, they withdrew to one side to bathe, dipping their heads forward into the water, lifting them high and splashing water over their backs; after which they flopped their wings and dipped into the water again. Once clean, they drifted back toward the pipe for more offal.

Now that Sewall could move about, we began to take part in the social life of the colony—movies, dinners, cocktail parties, and teas.

Most of the guests were government officials and their wives, who had come out from England on contract and could hardly wait to return. The government of the islands consisted of the Governor, appointed by the Queen, and a Legislative Council, the majority elected by the people, the rest appointed by the Governor. On paper this looked ideal; in practice, it didn't work. Invariably the Governor was forced to appoint members for districts that were unable to vote because of the weather or lack of candidates. Farmers resented having to attend its meetings in Stanley, where storms might hold them up for weeks; they also resented Stanley, referring to it as a necessary evil, a parasite of the colony, or worse. Consequently the Governor controlled "Legco," as it was called. The officials, sent by the Colonial Office in London, were responsible for public utilities, schools, medical service, roads, and public buildings. The road commissioner was not fired even though the roads were so bad that the springs and tires in cars had to be replaced every five thousand miles; the water commissioner kept his job even though twenty dead sheep were found in the ditches leading to the reservoir. The Falklanders endured all this passively.

Everyone was extremely kind to us, but I felt an undercurrent of discontent beneath the surface. The majority of the English officials and their wives were waiting for the day they could go home; they never tried to like the Falklanders or the islands. They hated the cold and the boredom, the town and the camp. Most of them had never been outside Stanley.

"Haven't you ever seen the penguins?" I asked the wife of one official, after we had sat through some dreary films, all that the *Fitzroy* had brought on its last trip.

"Only Pengy at the Cawkells'," she said in a tone that implied one penguin was enough.

That evening, the director of the wireless station drove us home. "My wife was the only Falklander there tonight," he explained after he had dropped her at their door. "She feels a bit awkward among government people, though she's been to England. We're going back there to live when my term expires," he added quickly.

I was annoyed. His wife was attractive and well-dressed; why should she have felt out of place? Yet I found that Falklanders were often on the defensive, waiting to hear how much we disliked their islands. I wanted to defend them. Four weeks ago I would have been overjoyed to go home. Now I liked it here.

Shortly after, we were guests at a tea, over Sewall's protests. He felt we should be out photographing; the afternoon light was the best of the day. But he warmed up over tea and scones in front of the fire in the drawing room, and even became enthusiastic when our host Mr. Barton, the F.I.C. manager, told us that the *Fitzroy* was scheduled to leave Stanley on December 12 for a trip around the camp. She would stop at the larger farms and some of the islands, and there would be plenty of chances for photography.

"You might even see a seal snatch a penguin," Mrs. Barton said. "Sometimes they'll catch a baby penguin on land and take it into the water and shake it so hard the penguin pops out of its skin. I've seen them."

The Bartons and several other friends walked home with us to see Pengy take his daily swim in the harbor. His habit was to porpoise about in the water for a few minutes and then come ashore. This time he swam straight out and down the harbor without a backward glance and disappeared in the rough waves. We waited for some time, but he did not return.

"Off to South Georgia," Edwin sighed with a mixture of relief and regret.

Rowan burst into tears, and he tried to comfort her. "I'll call the wireless station and have them broadcast it at seven. He might land again somewhere around the harbor."

We did not have to wait until seven. Pengy landed at Government Jetty and rode home in Mr. Barton's car. Rowan insisted that he hung his head in shame, but he did not show any signs of remorse as he gobbled his supper of mutton tenderloin in the kitchen. Sometimes he took the pieces of meat from Edwin's hand; often he lifted them off the edge of the table; he never tried to retrieve any bits that fell on the floor. I had seen him leaning over to pick up or put down pebbles or bits of vegetation in the garden, but I never saw him taking food from the ground or the floor. Neither, we observed later, did the penguins in the gentoo colony.

For the next two weeks, we photographed gulls, stinkers, and skuas whenever there was activity at the slaughterhouse. In between we worked on robins and siskins or on black-throated finches. At the city dump they were so tame we needed no blinds, and the finches with their vivid plumage of green, blue, and yellow made beautiful pictures as they searched for dandelion and daisy seeds among the rusted tin cans and broken bottles; our only problem was to delete the background.

All the time we needled Dr. Slessor for permission to return to the camp. Three weeks after the accident, he gave in. When I said we would go back to Kidney Island, he said, "No, Charles Point, we can keep an eye on you there," and John Huckle concurred, having no taste for another midnight rescue expedition.

I nearly had to stamp my foot and scream to convince them that I could not take care of a one-armed man at Charles Point; living was easier on Kidney Island. They reluctantly agreed.

"But arrange a set of signals with the lighthouse keeper," John Huckle said.

A "tussock bog"—Kidney Island

Rockhopper nests in the tussock

Chapter 6

BACK TO THE PENGUINS

Now all we had to do was find a way to get to Kidney Island. The *Philomel* and the *Protector* were both in the camp. I was about to give up and settle for Charles Point and the *Stockfish* when the *Gambler,* a new fifty-four-foot cargo vessel, trim and fast, arrived from the South American coast. On Saturday, November 28, she took us back to Kidney Island.

For all our unpleasant memories of the place, landing on the beach that beautiful morning was like coming home. From his bed in the tussock the old sea lion placidly watched us unloading. Logger ducks and their broods paddled about in the shallow water. Jackass penguins crossing the beach paused momentarily before disappearing into the tussock. There were house wrens, robins, and tussockbirds everywhere.

All of it begged to be photographed. Impatiently we settled our gear in the hut, moving cautiously to protect Sewall's useless arm. Then we set out for the rockhopper colony through the swamp where we had cut a path. The birds apparently liked our trail; they had it so filled with their nests that we could hardly find a place to put a foot without stepping on an egg or a bird. The rockhoppers yacked as we approached; some of them remained firmly on their nests as we passed. When they jabbed at us, I felt like a gentoo running the gauntlet in slippery mud.

Once on the cliffs we had to walk along a knife-edged rock for about ten feet. On one side it dropped almost straight into the sea seventy-five feet below; on the other it sloped about five feet into a pool of murky water. The sight of Sewall balanced on it, his good hand carrying the heavy camera—the only one I could not lift—and the other in a sling, made me gasp.

73

Beyond the rock we found a sheltered cleft, a crevice about four feet wide at the base, where the upper part of the cliff had split off from the main rock of the island. On our left, as we faced north, was the sheer precipice with the nesting penguins; between us and the sea rose a broken, crumbling rock that was a sort of rockhopper club or lounging area. On our right, just over a little rise, was the cliff occupied by the king shags.

The place was fairly quiet now. All up and down the face of the cliff, rockhoppers sat on nests lodged precariously on narrow shelves formed where layers of rock had broken off the vertical strata. Here and there a few unoccupied mates hopped about gathering tussock grass for nesting material. We watched one bird go up and down the cliff dozens of times, moving all the grass from a deserted nest far down the cliff to its own above. It was a long trek. Often before it reached its destination, it lost the sprigs of grass and went back for more. When it reached its nest, it simply plunked the whole mouthful of grass right on the back of its sleeping mate, which never stirred. Each time it went down the cliff it acted as if it had never done it before, peering down nearsightedly to see what its feet were doing and carefully hopping from one narrow shelf to another. It hardly ever lost its footing or slipped even a short way.

As soon as we were settled in our narrow niche it became obvious that we were in the main path of the penguins coming in from the sea. They landed, it seemed, at the base of the cliffs, then scaled the steep rock and came up over the edge where we first saw them, clean and glossy. Here they rested a bit before descending into our niche and then climbing to the top of the main cliff. From there some went easily to their nests in the tussock; others scrambled down to nests on the almost vertical cliff. Sewall and the tripod startled them for a moment but did not deter them. They hesitated and then pushed on around the tripod, underneath it, and between the legs of the cameraman.

I could not see the area where the birds were landing, but I could tell by watching the penguins porpoising in the water that it was somewhere at the base of the cliff. I started for the cliff behind the idling rockhoppers.

"Come back before you break your neck," Sewall shouted, looking up. *"What* are you doing to those birds?"

Pandemonium had broken loose about my feet. Furious rock-hoppers were jumping all around me, throwing themselves at each other. The din was ear-splitting. Their black and yellow plumes stood up straight, their red eyes glared, flippers slapped, sharp bills jabbed.

"*I* didn't do anything," I shouted, trying to extricate myself.

"You upset the whole club!"

The racket subsided and the quarreling ceased. Each penguin, safe on its own shelf, relaxed into a drowsy lump and half closed its eyes.

Watching the rock where they lounged, we observed that although rockhoppers are gregarious, each bird prefers to keep a little space between itself and its neighbor. Ornithologists call this "individual distance." When a bird stepped aside for me it intruded on the space of another, which resented it and attacked. This started a chain reaction that ran the entire length of the rock. I was not the only one who disturbed the peace. A newly arrived penguin could stir up a commotion if it was careless of where it hopped. Sometimes a lone bird had a miserable time making its way through the lounging area; at other times a dozen birds hopped through unnoticed.

Now we knew what to do to set the birds in action. Whenever Sewall wanted to photograph irate penguins, I had only to walk to the end of the rock and push a sleepy bird.

When the weather was bad and the light uncertain, we worked on the beach where birds scurried about gathering food for extra mouths. Robins, house wrens, and tussockbirds followed us, collecting tiny crustaceans from beneath the rotting kelp we dislodged as we walked. On one tussock bog we found a robin's nest stuffed with well-grown young; on another a house wren's nest, deep inside; and a tussockbird's nest under a third. The owners, their mouths loaded with food, darted into the nests and shot out again as if they hadn't a moment to lose. Even the jackass penguins sped up their deliberate waddle across the beach and into the tussock where their young waited.

The logger ducks, heavy-bodied and slow-moving, were not photogenic, but their ducklings were more attractive. The female brooded the babies in the soft tussock grass on the edge of the beach while the male, with his head under his wing, snoozed on

a rock by the water. When we came too close, the female rose
slowly and led the ducklings across the beach to the water, making
muffled, urgent sounds. There the male would join them and the
family would float about just off shore. It was sad to see that
the brood grew smaller daily, the ducklings disappearing one by
one. It may have been the work of the kelp gulls that patrolled
the harbor, or of sea lions that were always lurking in the water.

*Logger ducks, ungainly flightless birds; unfortunately, the
young will soon look just like their parents*

The territories of the logger ducks were sharply defined. Two
families lived near our beach, one right by the path, the other
farther down the shore. In the other direction, beyond the sea
lion, was an area of rock and sand that was apparently the
property of all the unmated logger ducks in the vicinity. They
were never permitted to enter the territories of the mated pairs.
Sewall saw a hair-raising fight one day when a strange pair of
logger ducks swam into one family's territory; first the males
fought, then the females as well. Edwin had once described such
a fight in which one male drowned another in Stanley Harbour.
Here at Kidney Island when the intruders had retreated, the

victorious male, bleeding and spent, could hardly drag itself ashore.

Later, when we had a camera with us, we tried to incite a logger duck battle. Over and over I attempted to drive an unmated duck into family territory. I waded into the water, shouted, and threw rocks, but I could never force the bird beyond a certain point or get it close enough to arouse the master of the territory. It evaded me, swimming in a wide arc, with wings beating wildly, and invariably managed to return to its own beach.

Sewall wanted to check on the kelp geese he had been photographing when he broke his arm. I resisted, warily remembering precarious rocks where they nested, but finally gave in. When we came near the end of the point, we saw the two adults and their goslings, just out of the nest, moving slowly down the ledge to the sea.

Kelp geese and their young; the all-white bird is the male

The gander led the slow procession, stopping often to wait for the goose, hesitating at every step until each small gosling had caught up, then moving on and waiting again. Seven goslings with fluffy white down went in single file from one ledge down to the next, tumbling and sprawling, picking themselves up and tumbling again. At the lowest ledge, about a foot above the water, the launching began: the gander, then the goose, slid in, and the youngsters in turn dropped without hesitation into the water just as though they had done it many times before. Quickly the babies drew together to form a solid little raft and with the gander in the lead and the goose in the rear the flotilla was under way. Kelp geese are sea geese. They never migrate but spend their entire lives in one small area, never leaving the shore except to go to the edge of the tussock to nest.

Kelp geese and young; the original brood of seven has been reduced by the depradations of gulls and skuas

There was always action on the rockhopper cliffs. After the eggs were laid, the kelp gulls and skuas came; the gulls flew along parallel to the cliffs, seldom pausing. The skuas swung back and forth over the colony like evil spirits, watching for an unguarded egg. We never saw them destroy any, but we found eggs that had been pierced by a sharp bill, whether by gulls or skuas we could not be sure.

Sea lions swam leisurely below the cliffs. I recalled Mrs. Barton's stories and watched carefully to see if a sea lion would make a pass at a penguin, but the birds merely swam in circles around the huge beasts with no unhappy consequences.

One afternoon an unusually large number of penguins were porpoising about beneath the cliffs, zigzagging through the water, then disappearing. They seemed to be following schools of fish. Suddenly clouds of terns—Cassin's terns—appeared in the air above them, their silver wings flashing and they hovered, then dove. They were after the same school of fish as the penguins— a case, not unusual in nature, of one species helping another to find food.

Sewall tried to train his lens on the penguins plunging in and out of the water and the terns following them. Often his guess as to where the penguins would appear next was as good as the terns'. He kept the film whizzing through the camera; my cold fingers were all thumbs when I tried to change the film in a hurry and he became so impatient that when I went back to the hut for more film I brought the Leica for him to use while I was reloading. It was difficult and exacting work, and we stayed with it till sunset. The terns and penguins were still fishing when we left. The next time we came back to the cliffs, the terns had vanished and we never saw another in the Falkland Islands.

One day a family of logger ducks with five ducklings fed beneath the cliffs. When the adults dived, the youngsters dived too, slanting down through the clear water until they dissolved from our view. A moment later they rose straight up from the black depths and popped above the surface like so many gray bubbles.

There was so much to photograph that Sewall was completely distracted from the penguins. Finally he announced flatly that he was going to photograph nesting rockhoppers and nothing else, and that I wasn't even to notice any other birds. When we reached the colony and slid into our cleft, I heard him say, "For heaven's sake, what's *that* doing here?"

I peered around a tussock bog and saw an enormous brown bird sitting high on an old shag nest right on the edge of the penguin colony.

"That," Sewall said, "is a sooty albatross. It's not supposed to be here."

He took pictures from where we stood with the big lens; then I moved the camera closer, and he took more pictures with smaller lenses. Finally we were only four feet away. The sooty albatross was a handsome creature, all soft brownish-gray except for a white eye ring and a longitudinal yellow line on its highly polished black bill. It dwarfed the penguins and shags, but they ignored it.

"I must have stills of this," Sewall whispered, and I started back to the hut for the Leica. When I returned, Sewall was sitting on a worn-down tussock bog right beside the bird. They were just looking at each other, communing, perhaps, as only bird and ornithologist can.

This handsome sooty albatross was on
Kidney Island for three days

The sooty albatross stayed on the nest for three days. We moved past it to photograph the rockhoppers, and set the tripod right beside it when we worked on king shags. It watched us constantly but made no move to leave. The fourth day it was gone. Alone and displaced, it had probably left to look for familiar ground, perhaps to fly hundreds of miles north to Tristan da Cunha where the species nests.

In spite of these diversions the stack of films exposed on rock-hopper penguins was very impressive by the end of the week. On Friday, since there was a strong wind from the northwest, we decided to work on the protected beach, photographing small birds.

When we reached the edge of the bank we heard a clamor from below. The harbor was like a mill pond and the beach was alive with excited jackass penguins. Some were clustered in small groups, others were milling around, still others were trumpeting; a very few were motionless, merely watching. It looked as though the penguins were having a party.

Jackass penguins on the beach

The birds in the small groups were clicking bills, the way puffins do in the Northern Hemisphere. Two birds would walk up to each other, put their heads together as if exchanging secrets, then click their bills together faster and faster. They were joined by others until there were six or eight in a circle, all leaning toward the center clicking bills madly. Then suddenly they all raised their heads and walked away, possibly to form other groups.

The more extroverted birds were trumpeting—a process that involved the whole penguin. A bird about to trumpet puffed itself full of air, held its head and bill straight up, and like a bellows emitted the air in a series of gusts that produced the most doleful braying sounds, quite inconsistent with the spirit of a beach party. Each trumpeter attracted other penguins, which gathered around it as if to marvel that so much noise could come from one of their number. We heard these noises at night from the tussock; they were blood-curdling and fearful in the dark, but ridiculous in the sunshine.

Every so often a few penguins decided to go for a swim. They waded into the water up to their flippers, bent down slowly, and were away in a flash. From where we stood on the top of the cliff their black bodies showed up clearly against the sandy bottom and we were aware of a metamorphosis. The clumsy bird that ambled into the water was transformed into a sleek black torpedo, darting about with incredible speed. The flippers, once its wings, became propellers; its flat yellow feet acted as rudders. One group after another waddled into the water, shot straight out, circled several times, and returned to the beach. We admired their perfect streamlining and their festive air. They did not go into the water to feed or to bathe, but just to play, to enjoy being penguins.

When the *Gambler* came to pick us up Saturday, we asked the captain to row us to Kidney Cove on the mainland where we could photograph jackass penguins beside their burrows—something we couldn't do on tussock-covered Kidney Island.

He shook his head. He felt a storm coming on; the glass was falling; we must leave at once. Either he was a good weather prophet or just lucky. Before we reached Stanley a fierce wind and rain were buffeting the little ship, which pitched and tossed rather frighteningly. But regardless of the weather, we felt triumphant. Sewall was in one piece, we had some good pictures, and I could face four days at Charles Point without a tremor.

At Charles Point it seemed like summer. Even though the wind beat on us incessantly and the nights were cold, there were moments of bright sunshine and blue skies. The yard around the tin hut was carpeted with small English daisies, and the balsam bogs were masses of tiny white stars. Sand cabbage made a yellow fringe around the beach at Rabbit Cove. Its limited ecological niche was only a slender band between the high tide mark and the grassy bank of the upland.

There was a family of Falkland plovers in the sand cabbage. The very small precocial young ones scampered about so fast that they looked like rolling marbles. When they "froze," as the chicks of shore birds often do, they faded into the sand and we had to look hard to find them. While we searched, the adults tried to distract our attention from the chicks by flopping around as if their wings were broken.

We found the lovely nest of a black-throated finch, tucked cozily under a diddle-dee bush in the center of a hummock of grass that rose from a shallow tea-colored pool in a peat bog.

A gentoo parent and its still downy offspring

The gentoo colony on the bluff at Arrow Point was one big hatchery; eggs were breaking open in every nest. And never were there such chicks. Compared to the adults they were very small, only about four inches high, and covered with a short silvery-gray down so thick and soft and glossy that it looked like plush. Their heads were a darker gray and their eyes, feet, and bills were black.

They looked quite delicate, but actually they were very tough. They had to be; their parents showed little concern for their feelings. They plunked their great orange feet right down on the helpless little things so that I expected them to be crushed. Instead, when the foot was lifted, the chicks sprang up as perky as before.

We had been here first on October 24 and the birds were just beginning to lay. Now it was December 7 and the eggs were hatching. That made the incubation period about six weeks—just right, according to the book.

Although there were no gulls or skuas near the colony, the young penguins were nevertheless closely guarded. One parent was always at the nest, which usually held two young, one somewhat older than the other. The chicks were fed by the other parent when it returned from the sea. The adult leaned over the little bird and literally poured food into its open mouth. The food looked like bright pink mush; it consisted of tiny pelagic shrimps, animals that swim just beneath the surface of the sea. The chicks were often so stuffed with them that they stood rigid, with stomachs distended almost to the bursting point.

They grew fast and within three or four days after hatching the plushy natal down was forced out by a second growth of thick, fluffy down more like fur than feathers. The new growth was all light gray except for a white front.

The chicks often stood up, stretched, and waved their little flippers but showed no inclination to walk or leave the nest. Most of the day they slept. When we came near, they sometimes crept between the legs of the adult and peered out from under its white feathers.

Both the adults and young were pestered at times by hooligans, unmated birds that roamed the colony, snatching nesting material and attempting to brood the young. These rowdies were generally sent on their way in a hurry with jabs and pinches.

All day the birds came to and from the colony, exchanging the duties of nesting and feeding the young; but during the late afternoon birds streamed in a steady procession over the ridge from the sea, and few if any left the colony. By sunset there were two birds attending almost every nest.

A gentoo and its young

After watching the gentoos for a few days, I decided they were mischievous and sly. They could jab angrily at a passer-by and by the time the bird had turned around, be settled comfortably back on their nests as if they hadn't moved for hours. They could beat each other cruelly with flippers at one moment, and stroll off with total disinterest the next. One of them would pinch a neighbor's chick on one side and poke affectionately at its own on the other. As for stealing nesting material, the art improved each day. However devilish it was, a gentoo always managed to maintain an air of gentle innocence. Whenever there was a scuffle I half expected the guilty party to look up and say, "Who, me?" Whether they were porpoising in the harbor, landing on the beach, plodding up the grass path, feeding young, stealing diddle-dee, or raising their heads to trumpet, the gentoos had great charm.

Mollymawk and young

Chapter 7

AROUND THE CAMP

At midnight on December 11 we boarded the *Fitzroy* for a trip around the camp and were installed in the same snug cabin we had occupied on the voyage from Montevideo. We sailed early the next morning, and after breakfast, in bright sun and brisk wind, we watched the mountains of East Falkland glide by. By midmorning the mountains had disappeared, and the rest of the way down the east coast the land was flat—so flat that when the clouds closed in making the sky and water gray, the coast was only a thin, sometimes imperceptible ribbon between sea and clouds.

Mary Cawkell was writing a history of the Falkland Islands, and in preparation for the trip I borrowed the manuscript and read it. The Falklands, discovered in 1592 by the Englishman John Davis, master of the ship *Desire,* were named for Lord Falkland in 1690. In the eighteenth and nineteenth centuries, British possession was disputed by the French, Spanish, and Argentines, and the Argentines still lay claim to them. The claimants expelled each other, or withdrew voluntarily from time to time. In 1831 the United States battleship *Lexington* destroyed the Argentine settlement of Soledad while protecting American vessels in Falkland waters. By 1833 the British held firm possession and the islands were incorporated into the Empire. They hardly appear in history again until 1914 when the British Navy destroyed the German Pacific Fleet in the Battle of the Falkland Islands.

The early settlers had no native population to subdue, but they had to struggle to eke an existence out of the cruel, barren islands. Their cattle escaped and ran wild, and the gauchos from the Argentine came over to hunt them. Charles Darwin joined

one such hunt; he had a low opinion of the islands. By the early
nineteenth century they were a lawless no man's land ruled by
violence and murder. The smaller western islands were used as
outposts by whalers and sealers when they went south to Antarctica; they left goats, pigs, and poultry and planted gardens to
assure them a food supply on the northbound voyage. Ships
rounding the Horn put in for repairs and to replenish their food
and water.

When the islands became part of the British Empire, order
was established, the capital built at Stanley, and new settlers,
mostly farmers, began to arrive. The whalers found South Georgia
a more convenient base; the wild cattle almost disappeared and
traffic around the Horn diminished. Sheep farming became the
principal industry and the islands, more isolated than ever,
prospered quietly on wool and postage stamps.

It was rough the first day out. Sewall forgot to take his dramamine pills and did not feel like having tea; but I had mine with
the three other passengers who were making the entire trip around
the camp: Mr. Young, director of the Falkland Islands Company
in London; Mr. Mortimer, a physicist from the ionospheric station
in Stanley; and Mr. Bell, a wool expert from Punta Arenas, Chile,
and London. Mr. Young and Mr. Mortimer were very agreeable,
but Mr. Bell obviously disliked Americans and began to bait me.
He described the atrocious behavior of G.I.'s in London during
the war, and when I didn't respond to that, he made fun of the
Texas oil men who were stationed at Punta Arenas.

To calm my rising irritation at his remarks, I walked briskly
around the deck several times after tea. The weather was steadily
growing worse; the wind howled under an ominous sky and the
ship dipped and dived as we crossed Falkland Sound. By dinner-
time the rails were on the tables. We went on deck again to see
the two great prominences, East and West Fox Bay Heads, that
marked the entrance to Fox Bay. On the eastern side a spectacular
colony of king shags swept up the cliff.

At dusk, about nine-thirty, we came in sight of the houses and
outbuildings of Fox Bay East nestled together in a valley surrounded by low rolling hills. The *Fitzroy* pulled quietly up to
the jetty and suddenly sprang to life: cranes and cables swung
in the wind, the gangplank was slapped down, passengers hunted
for baggage.

Edwin had briefed us on the proper behavior at ports of call: "This is a business trip for the *Fitzroy* and no concessions are made to the passengers. When she anchors at a settlement and the launch goes ashore you may go too, but you must be ready to return with it. The launch will never wait for you, and neither will the *Fitzroy*. Once she toots she's off, and if you miss her it might take you weeks, or even months, to get back to Stanley.

"You should wait for an invitation before going ashore. Some people have been alone so long they do not welcome guests. But if you have no invitation and there is something special you want to see, go ashore, present yourself to the manager, and ask permission to visit a bird colony, or collect mosses or look for pebbles, and he will give it."

Mary warned me to wear skirts whenever we went ashore; blue jeans and slacks were not acceptable. Soon I found, however, that it was perfectly proper to wear light rubber boots over thick socks, then remove the boots on arrival and walk about any house in stocking feet.

As the *Fitzroy* was being made fast, I noticed a small, trim woman on the jetty, calling and waving. Someone asked her whatever she was doing there.

"I guess I can come down to meet my own sister if I want to," she said. It was apparently the custom for women to wait in their homes for their guests, who had often been invited in advance by wireless. Mrs. Clement, wife of the manager of Fox Bay East, was the only woman we met on the whole trip who came to the jetty to meet the boat. She ran up the gangplank and welcomed her sister, who had been in England for a year, then turned to us and invited us to her house for a quick cup of tea. "We'll have to hurry," she said. "You'll be here less than two hours."

We followed her past the low, dark buildings at the head of the jetty to a big rambling white house that stood on a rise beyond it. Masses of roses and geraniums lined the conservatory where we removed our muddy boots. On one side there was a book-lined study, and on the other a large living room with an enormous peat fire and colorful slip-covered furniture. It seemed more like an English country house an hour's ride from London than a sheep farm in the South Atlantic.

Mr. Clement, torn between the pleasure of having company and his duties on the jetty, kept appearing and disappearing.

"Had a tough week," he said at one interval. "On Wednesday we heard over the wireless that the Governor was coming here for lunch. What do you suppose I had to do, right in the middle of shearing, with the shed crammed full? I had to get dressed up and row out to meet the plane. And who was on it? Huckle and the pilot. Upset my whole week."

He carried in a pile of books and magazines that the *Fitzroy* had brought. "I always get my copies of *Time*," he said with satisfaction. "The Colony Club in Stanley can't make *Time* understand their address. Their copies go to Buenos Aires and are burned."

He went out and came back at eleven-thirty with the news that the terrific gale had stopped the unloading of the *Fitzroy*.

"Wonderful," Mrs. Clement said. "That means you'll be here overnight and can come to breakfast in the morning—nine o'clock sharp. We eat late on Sunday. No excuses," she added as she saw me about to demur.

The crew of the *Fitzroy* worked by the weather, and the next morning they awakened us when they started unloading again before five o'clock. At nine we sat down to breakfast at the Clements' at a massive oak table covered with a blue and white cloth and set with blue pottery and lovely silver. At one end two great platters of bacon and eggs were kept sizzling hot over alcohol burners while we ate our porridge. There were heaps of toasted homemade bread, bowls of marmalade, and the best coffee we had had in six weeks.

The telephone rang all through breakfast. West Falkland had its own telephone system, which often broke down but was functioning in high gear this morning. Friends and relatives sixty or a hundred miles away rang up to welcome Mrs. Clement's sister. We had a phone call too—an invitation from Dr. Szeley, West Falkland's only physician, to have "smoko" at his house at eleven. He would call for us.

Meanwhile the pre-teen-age Clement girls and their cousin, a boy of ten, showed us the conservatory. Besides roses and geraniums, vegetables grew here, sturdy plants with small green tomatoes, cucumber vines in blossom, and radishes and lettuce.

The children were enthusiastic horseback riders; each had her own horse and gear. The whole family was planning to ride to Port Howard for a Christmas house party. House parties were an institution in the Falklands, at Christmas, Sports Day, and in slack seasons, as between shearing and dipping. They lasted for a week or more, with dances every night in the cookhouse and sports of all kinds during the day. It took nearly all year to get ready for the hordes of guests who would ride from great distances to attend a house party.

The cousin had just returned from his first term of school in Stanley, and was staying with the Clements until his father could send horses for him to ride to his home forty miles away. He disliked school after the casual atmosphere of the camp where lessons were taught by mothers or anyone else who happened to be around. The girls studied every morning with the wife of the wireless operator as teacher; but the "traveling teacher" was coming soon to bring them new books and give them examinations. He might stay two weeks or a month, depending on the weather and how soon he could get transportation to the next farm.

Dr. Szeley arrived and we walked to his house in the government enclosure that contained, besides his own, the homes of the wireless operator and a caretaker. It was a two-story building, comfortably furnished by the government, and also served as his surgery.

The doctor and his wife, both Hungarian refugees, were a charming young couple, who had taken a post that few Englishmen care to accept. City-bred, they had adapted themselves well, not only to new language and customs, but to the rigors of country life in unremitting cold and wind. They had learned to ride horseback, plant gardens, raise chickens and pigs, and shoot wild fowl. While her husband traveled endless miles by horse, boat, and plane, Mrs. Szeley busied herself keeping house, sewing, and knitting. Now their three-year term was almost up and they were ready to go. They had had enough of wind, peat, mutton, and cold.

"And the conversations," the doctor added. "Always the same—of sheep, horses, and dogs." The medical experience was limited too. He cared for five hundred people, some of whom lived a hundred miles away. Very sick patients were sent to Stanley, weather permitting; he could follow their cases only by talking to Dr. Slessor by wireless. It was hardly the way to hold confidential conversations.

"Dr. Slessor speaks excellent German, so we tried that, but we had to stop. Complaints came from all over the camp. People said they weren't going to have 'Nazi' spoken over their wireless. What really made them mad was missing all the clinical details."

Mrs. Szeley brought smoko—tea and cookies. Smoko originated in the wool sheds in Australia. Because of the danger of fire amid the grease-laden wool, smoking was forbidden in the shed during the shearing season; so at ten each morning the men went outside for a smoke. When tea and cakes were added, smoko became the morning tea break, and the custom continued and spread.

Freddy White joined us at noon and told us that the unloading had been called off again and all of the passengers were to go with him to the Clements' for supper. In the afternoon Sewall and I went back to the ship and took storm pictures from the deck. Great black clouds swept down across the bay from the hills above Fox Bay West with blasts of snow, sleet, and rain. Sometimes the squalls missed the ship; more often they struck full force, swirling through her ropes and rigging, slamming her hard against the jetty one moment, and straining her land lines the next. All afternoon I adjusted lenses and wiped them, changed films, covered and uncovered the cameras, and served as an anchor for the tripod so that the whole outfit would not be swept away. We did not even stop for tea. Finally, wet, cold, and desperately tired, we put away the cameras just in time to dress for supper ashore.

Supper at the Clements' was bountiful and delicious. Besides clear soup, cold mutton and beef, a fresh green salad, and chocolate pudding (the kind one had before package mixes were invented) there was a surprise—a Falkland pie. Mrs. Clement gave me the recipe: "Half fry lots of bacon. I don't know how much—just lots. In a large baking dish break some eggs—about twenty, maybe. Alternate layers of bacon with eggs. Partially bake in a moderate oven. When the eggs are set, put a pastry crust on the top and finish baking. The seasoning you must do for yourself. Of course if you have a few bits of boiled brains or tongue it will be that much better. Serve cold."

My memory of the Falklands is largely of endless, unrelenting wind, but of all we experienced there, the blast that tried to block our return to the ship that night was the worst. The six of us clung to each other, leaned against it like a wall, and forced our way down the hill and along the jetty; then Sewall and I, grasping the rail, pushed toward the aft cabin. The *Fitzroy* rolled and bumped all night long in the bay as if it were open sea.

By morning the wind had slackened. While the *Fitzroy* began unloading for the third time, we went with Mr. Young by launch to Fox Bay West, one of the larger F.I.C. farms, with a population of about sixty, and a brand new twenty-seven-room prefabricated house in manor style for the manager and guests. We made a tour of the wool shed and the cookhouse, which housed the single men and was the social center of the community, serving as school, dance hall, movie theater, and church. Suddenly a call from the jetty told us that the *Fitzroy* was, by this time, unloaded, and we went back across the bay in the launch, our feet resting on cases of gin that Mr. Young had got from the manager because the supply in Stanley was low and Christmas was near.

Once out of Falkland Sound we sailed west past sheer cliffs, some very high, all of them steep. Sometimes we sailed between the cliffs and great jagged upthrusts of rock. At night we entered an inlet and anchored among some small islands.

We awoke the next morning at Port Stephens; it was an enchanting day, cool and clear with only a hint of breeze. The ship lay in a fiord; mountains loomed on every side. High on a hillside was the manager's house; below it, along the slope to the harbor, were shepherds' houses, the cookhouse, wool shed, and pens. White houses with red roofs, set off by hedges of yellow gorse in full bloom, bright blue sea and sky—everything was vivid that sparkling morning. Even the paddocks seemed unusually green.

Sewall, Mr. Mortimer, and I went ashore and climbed to a cairn on a hill above the settlement. Across the fiord we could see several large stone runs, with tributaries of worn boulders joining the main stream that increased in size as it neared the sea. On the side of the mountain across the bay a great circle of gorse glowed like a sunburst.

We walked down behind the manager's house and came upon

the forest, a tangled mass of twisted evergreens tightly fenced. We found a gate and made our way down a path so narrow that the gnarled branches met overhead. Robins nested there as they did everywhere in the Falklands where there were trees.

In a paddock outside the forest a pair of wild upland geese grazed, quite unaware of us. It was our first good view of them, although we had seen many at a distance on the coast islands. They were somewhat longer-legged than kelp geese and had a rangier gate. The male's head, neck, and breast were pure white; his back and wings gray, barred on the back and flanks. The female was reddish brown with barred breast. Upland geese are good eating (later we had a gosling pie, like tender young chicken); but they forage on the grass that is so precious for sheep, and there is a bounty on them. In shepherds' homes we saw long strings of beaks that would be exchanged for government pennies. The upland geese, as easy to kill as barnyard fowl, may well be extinct before the government realizes that with proper management they could provide an excellent supplement to the monotonous mutton diet.

Four shepherds rode across the tract toward us, dressed in loose-fitting pants—"bombaches"—high boots, and berets, and sitting easily in their skin-covered western-style saddles. They were returning from the "gathering," their dogs trotting happily beside them. As soon as the *Fitzroy* left shearing would begin.

We heard a warning toot from the ship and hurried to the jetty where the men were still loading wool, in huge eight-hundred-pound bales. They nudged them down the sloping jetty and onto a barge with iron hooks; when the barge drew alongside the ship, the bales were swung aloft by cranes and lowered into the hold.

Our next stop was New Island, which we reached just before dark. We had no invitation, but we had a pretext for a visit— Christmas presents from the Cawkells to the Davises, the family with whom we were to spend the month of January. The wireless operator could get no reply from New Island and was going ashore to see what was wrong with their wireless.

Just as the launch left the ship, lights blinked on in the houses and men emerged and ran toward the jetty. After meeting Mr. Davis, we followed the wireless operator up the steep rise to the Davis house. Mrs. Davis and her two children, and Grandpa, an elderly man sitting in a chair with two canes beside him, greeted us, and soon we were chatting like old friends and making plans for our visit the following month.

It was pitch dark when we returned to the ship. I went to bed and had been asleep for about two hours when Sewall woke me. I sensed that something must be wrong. "There's no wind," I mumbled.

"But there's fog." He opened the door and I looked out at the searchlight illuminating the aft deck, and at myriads, clouds of birds that swarmed about it like giant moths, beating so furiously against the light that they dropped senseless to the deck and the barges below.

Sewall picked up a small silvery-gray petrel. "Slender-billed whalebird," he said, struggling with his clothes. "Fix my sling so I can go out."

I fell back a moment and was asleep again. The next time I opened my eyes he stood in the doorway holding the limp body of a large brown bird.

"Skua," he said. "They aren't supposed to travel at night. But this one was chasing petrels and crashed into our cabin door." He laid it on the shelf.

The next morning the crew was busy picking up numb, frightened whalebirds from every nook and cranny of the *Fitzroy*. I watched the assistant engineer fish a couple out from under a plank and toss them into the air. They flew away.

"Does this happen often?" I asked.

"As often as we hit New Island or hereabouts on a quiet, foggy night in spring or summer. You been around long enough to know it ain't often."

That put me in my place. Then he repeated the tales the whalers used to tell of how thousands of these birds were attracted to their bonfires and committed suicide in the flames. They were sometimes called firebirds. "Weren't many killed last night," he added, "Only stunned."

Enough were killed, however, and a good many of them lay beside the skua on our shelf. Once again our cabin became a laboratory. The crew brought in a box for a skinning table and placed it smack in the doorway. Then they gathered around to watch the process of removing the skin and stuffing it with cotton. For the rest of the trip there were birds to skin. When the fire-

birds were finished, the men brought others. At every stop they
"found" specimens, and I suspected that the death was not always
accidental. Sewall was delighted with the gift of a pair of upland
geese; because I refused to have them in the cabin he hung
them outside the door. When we next saw them the bills had
been neatly snipped off—collected for the bounty. As specimens
they were worthless, and the crew had them for dinner.

At Dunnose Head a beautiful brown and white horse bound for
West Point Island was brought aboard. It had to be coaxed to
walk down slanting planks from the jetty to the barge; once alongside the ship, a broad band was fastened around its belly, and the
horse, pawing the air desperately, was swung high and deposited
above the forward hold. There it had company, for the sheep
which had come with us from Montevideo and had been held in
quarantine in Stanley were also aboard.

At Roy Cove on December 17 it was gray and cold, and the
wind whistled in the rigging. I dressed without enthusiasm in my
warmest clothes and we waded through ankle-deep mud to the
home of the manager for breakfast.

Freddy and our fellow passengers were already there, standing
close to the fire in the drawing room with glasses in their hands.

"And now," our host said, "a gin and tonic for Mrs. Pettingill."
He handed me a glass. It seemed a little early in the day for a
gin and tonic, but after all it was my birthday. The drink tasted
very good at that hour on a gloomy morning.

The breakfast, served by a maid in uniform, was lavish. I sat
and stared at the three kinds of eggs—hens', penguins' and
mollymawks'. The mollymawk eggs were big enough to fill a
soup plate.

As we approached Chartres, land was close on both sides. In
some places there were hills that sloped gently from white beaches
to a height of six or seven hundred feet; in other places steep
cliffs. Beneath one cliff we saw two tight circles of birds floating
with the tide. They were blue-eyed shags, the assistant engineer
said, and they were fishing. Suddenly they dived, all of them at
once. Sewall had never heard of their rafting in this formation,
and consulted all his books, but not even his Bible, Murphy's
Oceanic Birds of South America, contained any reference to such
behavior.

Small tussock islands appeared here and there in the path of the ship, and speed was reduced to a crawl. We were entering at rising half tide so that if the ship got stuck on a sand bar the tide would lift her off.

That night the tide was unusually low and the *Fitzroy* was left stranded in the mud. But in the morning the ship was afloat again.

As we entered the mountain-encircled harbor of West Point the sun came out in a cloudless sky; the air was crisp; the whole world glittered.

We put ashore in the launch. "One hour," the first mate warned us as we landed and a tweedy gentleman came to meet us on the beach.

"One hour!" he exclaimed. "Freddy will just have to wait. You must see the bird colonies and the gardens. I'm Mr. Napier. Welcome to West Point."

He led us up the hill to a low house that was almost hidden by masses of evergreens and gorse. Behind them were gardens, tiny little plots boxed by high hedges, and radiant with the tallest, most brilliant lupines we had ever seen. Paths between the plots were bordered by fuchsias so high they met overhead and formed tunnels from the top of which the bell-like rose and purple blossoms dripped. While we stood breathless, Mrs. Napier, a tiny elf-like lady came upon us.

"I wish you might have seen them before the rain hit yesterday," she said. "You're the bird people, aren't you. You must go right along and see the penguins. Be sure and come back in time for a cup of tea." She gave us directions to the nearest bird colony and accompanied by Mr. Mortimer we set off.

The colony was on the far side of the island where the land fell away in a series of sheer cliffs. There were thousands of rockhopper penguins all up and down the cliffs, and their young too, tiny black chicks with white fronts. Mr. Mortimer was beside himself with excitement; it was the first penguin colony he'd seen. He rushed right in with a camera, and before I could warn him an angry, startled penguin had him by the leg. I was so concerned with him that I did not notice the mollymawks, great white birds with black wings, until Sewall called to me.

Then I wondered how I could have missed them. They sat on

high clay-colored chimney nests all in among the rockhoppers, dignified, aloof and superior, literally looking down their beaks at the fussy little penguins that bustled noisily beneath them.

Sewall was curious to know whether the mollymawks were sitting on eggs or brooding chicks. From a safe distance we watched him try to persuade one mollymawk to leave its nest or at least stand up. He waved his good arm to shoo it, but the bird just sat. When he walked around to push it from the rear, the bird turned on the nest without rising. The snapping of its razor-edge, four-inch-long bill deterred Sewall, who had forgotten his heavy gloves, from manhandling the stubborn creature; and Mr. Mortimer, having experienced the wrath of a small penguin, was in no mood to tangle with an albatross which had a wing spread of seven feet.

Returning to the settlement we saw Mr. Young and Mrs. Napier beside the paddock where the new horse grazed. West Point Island was so beautiful that morning I would gladly have been left behind. But Freddy waited long enough for me to have tea with Mrs. Napier in her cozy kitchen-dining room.

"I don't have a maid," she said. "It only ties one down. I'd rather come and go as I please. Every day now I ride out to see the penguins. Did you like the penguins?" Before I could answer, she asked, "Don't you want to come here to take pictures? You may if you like. Carcass Island is better, though. Go ashore and see my daughter Kitty Bertrand at Carcass this afternoon. The birds are wonderful there. It's been a sanctuary for years."

The *Fitzroy* tooted. I said good-bye and ran to the beach where the men waited. As we shook hands with Mr. Napier, Mr Bell said, "I may see you before I leave. I'll be in Stanley until January."

Mr. Napier stared at him. "You'll not see me in Stanley. I just came home from there two years ago."

We went ashore at Carcass that afternoon loaded with gear. I had cameras and lenses strung around my neck; both hands were full of films and gadgets. Too late I remembered the tripod we needed to support the big lens. It was back on the ship. Sewall was annoyed until he looked at me, "You're just the right height," he said. "Your shoulder will do." So I served as a tripod all afternoon.

The place was alive with birds—black and white oystercatchers, gray ducks, logger ducks, and black-crowned night herons on the beach; robins, red-breasted troupials, tussockbirds, and black-chinned siskins about the houses. We worked first on the gray ducks that came to the mouth of a small stream to feed. Floating in the very shallow water, they danced a jig, beating their feet back and forth to stir up mud and sand. Then they dipped down to collect any food they had uncovered. One pair did this over and over in unison.

Black and white oystercatchers

We turned to the oystercatchers, hopping about stiff-legged on a grassy bank, with their tails up over their backs like little fans. They led us to a ditch where a Paraguayan snipe was feeding, probing in soft mud beside a trickle of water.

When the film was gone, we had tea with the owner, Mr. Bertrand, and his wife Kitty, Mrs. Napier's daughter, at a long table drawn close to a window from which we had a good view of the harbor. Tussockbirds, used to coming to the window sills for crumbs, found the windows open and hopped right into the room. A big yellow cat curled up on a chair never so much as lifted a whisker.

"First cat on Carcass in many a year," Kitty said. "He's so old the birds are safe."

The previous owners of Carcass had never permitted a cat or a gun on the island. As a result the birds were abundant and very tame. The other farmers mentioned Carcass with pride, but it never occurred to them they could use the same conservation measures on their farms.

We spent our last night aboard off Port San Carlos, going ashore in the evening for a gay party in a relaxed and casual household, talking with our hosts of theater, politics and books. The long drawing room was crammed with books and magazines —only the overflow from the library; soon the owner was going to build a new house where there would be plenty of room for books and children. This couple, like most of the owners and managers of sheep farms, went to England for six months' holiday every three years; it was fun to go, they said, but wonderful to come back to the islands.

We had a delightful evening. Mr. Bell's anti-Americanism abated and when he returned to the ship he was so mellow that he sang "The Star Spangled Banner" down our ventilator.

The next day when we anchored off Ajax Bay more passengers came aboard, bound for Stanley for the Christmas holidays. Christmas was only two days off. It did not seem possible with the sun so high, the lupines so bright on West Point Island, the days so long.

The captain entertained us with gin and tonic before lunch, and we sat on his deck in the sun and watched the now docile sea reflect the headlands of the north coast. How alive the islands are, I thought, despite their isolation. In eleven days we had seen no other ship in open water; except for birds, whales, and porpoises, we had seen no life outside the settlements. Yet I had not met one person who was bored or restless. The camp, which so many considered empty, barren and lonely, actually had so much.

CHRISTMAS

Back at the Cawkells' it looked a bit like Christmas. A few cards brightened the living room mantelpiece, and a string of telegrams from the camp hung almost to the floor. It was the custom to exchange greetings by telegram instead of sending Christmas cards that might not be delivered for weeks. We had received just one Christmas card. I felt a little depressed, but we had no time for moping. The *Fitzroy* was leaving Stanley on December 29 and we had film to pack, scenarios to compose, and letters to write, all before Christmas. A long weekend lay ahead; with Sunday falling between two Sports Days, everything would be closed from Thursday until Tuesday.

In the Government Forest we found the siskin's nest full of well-grown young, and photographed it at once. Then we arranged for lodgings at the Ship Hotel—the Cawkells would be leaving soon for England—completed our shopping, and wrapped gifts.

Stanley was full of people in holiday mood. Whole families rode in on horseback; the plane brought others. The *Protector,* the *Gambler,* and the *Philomel* all came home bringing more guests, and the *John Biscoe* arrived from South Georgia. The days were crowded with social events: cocktails here, tea there, sherry at Government House after the Queen's speech, supper and a cinema on the frigate, drinks before the Sports Days races, luncheons between races, dances after races.

The day before Christmas we decorated Rowan's Christmas tree—a mere sprig of evergreen about three feet high—down to the last needle, then draped twisted strips of pastel crepe paper in garlands about the living room. Mary made the house bloom with pansies, primroses, veronica, and gorse. The day was so warm and pleasant that it seemed more like Easter.

Dressed in light summer cottons, wearing rubber boots, and carrying our best shoes in brown paper bags under our arms, we set out for tea. Our hosts, native Falklanders, served a huge Christmas cake, a confection that had been advertised over the radio for weeks in advance: a large round cake, covered with white icing, and decorated with sprigs of artificial holly and tiny Christmas bells, and surrounded by a band of gold foil with a red crepe-paper fringe. On cutting, it turned out to be a heavy dark fruit cake, the kind that would keep for weeks and could be served throughout the holidays. For a while we felt at home. Then we moved on to another house for dinner and Christmas Eve in the company of people who were, like us, exiles, crushing down thoughts of home. While we drank a sitting toast to absent friends, sunlight flooded the room decorated with bouquets of roses and paper streamers. There was no snow, no caroling, no Santa Claus, not even a crèche.

On Christmas morning the wind lashed across the harbor, driving sheets of rain against the house. A fire burned in the dining room during breakfast, and after Edwin had lighted the tiny candles on the evergreens bough, gifts were opened—some of them local substitutes for presents that had not arrived from England.

That afternoon we met some young men from FIDS—the Falkland Islands Dependency Survey. They were scientists who had manned or were about to man stations so remote and so desolate that Stanley seemed a metropolis by comparison. I thought that a year or two alone, or almost alone, on a barren, frozen island would change even the most normal men into morose, anti-social characters; but the room was full of ordinary English lads with perfect poise. I could not tell those who were coming home from those who were going down, except that the former spoke glowingly of the South and the latter listened intently. Those who had lived in the Antarctic corroborated what Shackleton had said— they had not been half so cold there as they were in Stanley in street clothes.

The Dependencies, like the Falklands, were claimed by both the British and the Argentines. The British maintained research stations, while the Argentines made occasional visits. We had read before we came to the Falklands of an international incident: the "expulsion" of the Argentines from a weather station in the Dependencies. One of the men told us, "We hadn't expected much resistance, but we were surprised when they just begged to be taken off. I've never seen men so happy to be expelled."

On Saturday, the first racing day, the sun was bright and the wind was only a breeze. The races took place in the Government Paddock adjacent to the Cawkells' back garden, and as we ate breakfast we watched cars rushing up and people on foot walking past the garden. Some of them looked in, walked on, hesitated, and looked again. Pengy stood right by the gate showing off.

Sewall spent the morning taking candid shots of the crowd with the Leica. I entered into the spirit of the occasion and bet on the horses, hanging over the paddock rail, running to the pay-off window, and exchanging tips with friends. My luck was good at first, but gradually ran out. There was only three fast horses and whenever they ran, everyone bet on them, and the pay-offs became smaller and smaller. Mary and I were reduced to making joint bets and finally ran out of money altogether.

After lunch, Sewall, assuming his "proper Bostonian" attitude, told me the holiday was over and we were going to make movies that afternoon. He was, he said, embarrassed at seeing me race from rail to betting window. So we spent four hours photographing the races and the gymkhana events, without even time off for tea or a gin and tonic at the temporary bar.

The last day of the races we moved to the Ship Hotel. Mr. Goodwin made two trips in the Land-Rover and our room was crammed with boxes, cases, and heaps of clothing. That evening we packed for New Island to the music of the dance at the Town Hall. Finally unable to resist it, we dressed for the dance, arriving in time to see the Governor award the cups and prizes for the day's events.

We wound up at the Colony Club in the early hours of the morning and said good-bye to everyone.

"We're off to New Island in the morning. We'll see you in a month."

They laughed and jeered. "That's what you think. We'll be saying good-bye to you for the next week—or next month."

But the next day was clear and bright. John Huckle phoned that the plane would leave at ten, and after stopping at Mr. Davis's mother's to collect messages, parcels, and a huge bouquet of roses for New Island, we boarded the Beaver and took off.

Rockhoppers launch themselves into the water from this stone ledge

Chapter 8

THE SEA-GIRT KINGDOM

New Island, the westernmost settlement in the Falklands, lay a hundred and fifty miles due west of Stanley. For the first ten minutes of flight we looked down on East Falkland—on mountains, rocks, inlets, and lakes, stretches of dark diddle-dee, patches of pale white grass, waterways bordered with green, broad rivers of gray stone. We saw no living things except scattered gray lumps that were sheep and white dots that were upland geese.

Halfway across East Falkland the weather closed in; snow and rain beat wildly against the little plane and the wind tossed us about so violently that I felt as if I were back in the Land-Rover.

When the clouds lifted we were over Falkland Sound. We crossed West Falkland; it was greener and less desolate, and its mountains were higher. Just beyond its western coast we dropped down and circled the Colliers, two huge upthrusts of rock that rose abruptly from ruffled collars of breaking surf. To the west, in bright sunshine, lay the mountainous crescent of New Island, described thus in *The South American Pilot:* "Vessels bound for any part of King George or Queen Charlotte bays, from the westward, should make New island, which cannot be mistaken, as it is the north-westernmost of the high cliffy islands which form the southwest portion of the Falkland group; and the lofty cliffs at its northwest points are very remarkable."

We flew over an arc of beach where the foam of breaking waves made white scallops on turquoise-blue water, over a lake that reflected the color of the sky, to the western shore. Then the plane veered north and flew close to sheer cliffs that stretched ahead on our right. Suddenly we turned eastward and swooped between two great walls. I shut my eyes. The pilot cut the motor

105

and the plane glided down and struck the water with a gentle lurch. When I opened my eyes we were bobbing about in a small bay.

From the jetty a dozen people waved, and a small boat, called a "pram," pulled away from it. In the stern sat Mr. Davis facing the oarsman, a heavy-set bearded man wearing a sailor suit and a beret. Mr. Davis introduced him as Jacob Goss. They tied the plane to the *Penguin,* the larger of the two schooners moored in the bay, and transferred our duffel to the deck. Then we lowered ourselves into the pram. Mr. Davis dropped the line of the Beaver, the propeller whirled, and the little plane rose and headed into a stormy eastern sky.

I worried about Sewall's climbing the slippery ladder to the top of the high jetty. His arm was out of the sling now, but Dr. Slessor had warned against pulling or lifting for at least two weeks. With Jacob's help it was no problem. Mrs. Davis and the children, Helen, nine, and Raymond, seven, met us, with two of the shepherds and their families; and still carrying the roses that Mrs. Davis had sent I walked with them up the hill to their house, a long, low stone building.

Grandpa and Hazel, the maid, greeted us in the kitchen and we went up a steep narrow staircase to the room that was to be ours. At the top of the stairs stood a brand new spinning wheel, which I glanced at longingly. I had always wanted to spin. From our room a dormer window looked out over Tigre Bay, and a small tidal island connected to the main island by a sand bar, a larger island in the mouth of the bay, and the shoulder of a mountain on the far side. Tussock covered the islands, and the gray mountain was strewn with rocks.

As I finished unpacking, Mrs. Davis called to me to walk to the garden with her. I shot down the stairs, giving my head a resounding whack on a low door frame, and reeled out along the track toward the jetty south of the house, past a small white building that was the store, and two one-story shepherds' houses, one new and covered with shiny metal, the other of wood painted white.

"The new house is Bob Keddle's—he's been here longest and Mally is expecting another baby," Mrs. Davis told me. "Tony and Winnie Felton and their little girl live in the old one. It's very comfortable and we'll not replace it for awhile yet."

Beyond the houses we turned right across the "rough sheep pasture" behind the shearing shed, and came to the garden that lay in a sort of fold at the foot of the mountain. There Mrs. Davis gathered mint from a small, neat plot. At the upper end of the garden were three trees and, sure enough, robins.

We were nine at the long table in the warm kitchen, for a special dinner—spring lamb and mint sauce. By the end of the meal we felt quite at home; New Island had made us welcome.

After dinner we cleared the table and collected an enormous platter of leavings. Agnes Davis showed me how to dispose of it. She went to the front garden, dumped the food on the ground, and banged on the empty plate with a spoon, calling "Here, kitty, kitty, kitty."

They came from all directions—big cats, little cats, yellow cats, black cats, and calico cats, together with multicolored chickens and a dog.

Jack Davis joined us. "There are about seventy-five cats," he told me. "We have to have them to keep down the firebirds and the jackass penguins. They'd undermine the island with their burrows if we didn't have plenty of cats." I noticed a number of pale, blue-gray wings scattered about in the dust. "They bring the firebirds in at night. When Grandpa first came they killed one right under his window. He thought it was a baby crying."

Jack leaned over to pat Old Stump, "the best sheep dog on the island," he said. Old Stump wagged what was left of his tail. A few cats played around him. They were pet cats, Agnes explained, and belong to members of the family. They were admitted to the house; other cats lived in the peat shed, and still others, "wild cats," resided in the camp. I asked how one distinguished the privileged cats from the others and remembered their names. "You learn," she said.

After Hazel had done the dishes, we all headed for the nearest bird colony, about a mile northwest of the settlement. The children pointed out the various buildings—a tremendous peat shed close to the house, and opposite it a wash house where Jacob lived; beyond, near the beach at the head of the bay where the path sloped down to the sea, stood the pigs' fattening house, several chicken coops, and a killing shed. The whole area was fenced and gated in a maze of pens and paddocks.

From the bay we turned west and walked up hill through a green valley, the "flat," to the cliffs of the western side where the surf had cut two great gullies. The plane had passed through one of them this morning as we approached New Island. All up and down the rock-studded sides of the gullies were thousands and thousands of birds. First we saw only rockhopper penguins. Then we spotted mollymawks among them, and here and there, in sub-divisions where the black and white birds seemed more closely packed, king shags. Raymond darted after a fat baby penguin, and his mother restrained him, warning him not to get nipped.

*Rockhopper penguins, king shags, and mollymawks nest in the
same areas, generally ignoring each other*

Leaving the children with Hazel, Agnes and I scrambled down the gully over the slippery ledges. Halfway down we paused to look at seals sleeping in the sun on the flat rocks, bulls and their mates—"clapmatches"—and females alone with pups of all sizes. We must have disturbed them, for two fierce males went into battle, puffing out their great manes and throwing themselves at each other with furious roars and mighty thrusts of flippers and jaws. Fascinated and terrified, we crouched low against the cliffs. The quarrel ended as abruptly as it began and the defeated bull, his yellow mane stained with blood, disappeared into the sea.

Far out the water boiled as a horde of porpoising birds approached a flat rock that slanted into the sea. A wave crashed in and suddenly about fifty penguins stood on the rock; another wave, and dozens more. The first arrivals hippity-hopped up the rock to a point where it dropped about four feet to a smooth ledge. Here they hesitated until the birds coming up from behind literally forced them to jump or be pushed. They paddled and hopped across the ledge keeping a proper distance from the indifferent sea lions, made another jump, and slowly began to trek up the rocky gully to their nests above. We could see them streaming up the trail in single file until the path forked and they split into two lines, some going north, the others south, still hopping in single file.

Like the gentoos they seemed to be activated by pressure from behind. At times a flock about to land became panicky and turned seaward to regroup and try again. They had to do it quickly because another group was already forming behind them. Once on the first rock they waited for new arrivals to push them off, and postponed the climb upward until the crowds behind forced them on. Each wave reminded me of the arrival of a commuters' train at a suburban station.

Agnes and I climbed around the cut, just above the sea lions, and joined the birds on their homeward path, upsetting their single-file procession. Agnes pointed out deep scratches and furrows in the hard rocks of the trail. The penguins were following the same path that their ancestors had followed for generations. How many penguin feet, over how many years, had it taken to scratch these rocks! When I told Sewall about them later, he smiled. "Those scratches have been reported before. The geologists tell us they are merely the result of water erosion." He was much more impressed with the landing rock as a place to photograph penguins.

The children brought us each a baby penguin to hold—the docile, fluffy rockhopper chicks were as soft as toys in Schwarz's Fifth Avenue window.

Around us were the remains of several small stone corrals about twenty feet in diameter with walls about two feet high. Whalers had built them, Jack told us, for herding penguins. When their oil tanks were not quite full they would drive the birds into the corrals, club them and press or boil them down for oil. They slaughtered them by the thousands.

Rockhopper penguins and young, still in the fuzzy, helpless stage

I looked at the orange and yellow cliffs dotted with birds, the steel-blue ocean, and the breaking surf. To the south rose Queen Victoria Mountain—"Old Vic." To the north were two mountains joined by a high rise. Westward stretched the wild sea driven by the incessant wind, pounding mercilessly against the cliffs, undercutting and eroding New Island. There was nothing between us and South America three hundred miles away.

We went home for tea. Then, leaving the children, Jack, Agnes, Sewall, and I set out on foot for the gentoo colony on Rookery Hill three miles north. I had managed to forestall the imminent proposal that I ride there on horseback. Armed with bamboo sticks from a chimney-cleaning rod (ordinary sticks were rare in the Falklands) we climbed toward the rise between the two mountains to the north. Beneath our feet the ground was pitted with the small burrows of the firebirds.

"Watch out," Agnes warned us. "Hold up your sticks." Before I·knew what was happening, several skuas attacked viciously from all sides, coming directly at us with the speed of sound. When they struck the sticks they circled and shot at us again while we plunged on.

"I used to think it was a joke about skuas," Jack said as we emerged from their nesting territory, "until one hit me right between the eyes. Drew blood. I had two black eyes for days."

When we reached the top of the ridge we stood breathless and gazed down the other side. We were on the rim of a great cirque at the bottom of which lay a large, island-dotted harbor—Ship Harbour. Grassy valleys and diddle-dee-covered ridges sloped from the rim downward to the white arc of a broad white beach. At the far end of it there was a cluster of black dots that Jack said were gentoo penguins.

"They always land on the same section of the shore," Agnes said, "but each year the location of the colony shifts a little. This year it's right on top of the mountain." We could see the tiny black and white figures plodding up the side of Rookery Hill.

We followed narrow sheep trails around the top of the cirque, over terrain broken by large burrows. Occasionally an occupant, a jackass penguin, stood by the opening; others labored up the slope from the sea. Upland geese grazed with the sheep on the hillside below us.

"Sheep down," Agnes said suddenly, and shot off toward a gray-brown hump that looked like an old stone. She tugged at it and righted it and a sheep ran away bleating.

"Just a habit here," Jack said, "watching for a sheep down. You get so you can spot one out of the corner of your eye. If one falls down when it's heavy with wool, it gets cast and can't get up. Then the skuas and turkey vultures move in and pluck out its eyes and tongue."

Agnes came back and pointed down to the New Island horses grazing in a green cut near the water. I knew what that would mean sooner or later.

Agnes and Jack outstripped us walking to the top of Rookery Hill to the colony on the western slope, and when I caught up with them Agnes was fondling a big, fat gray baby and burying her fingers in the thick down.

Rookery Hill was about seven hundred feet high, and I was

relieved when Sewall said that it was too far to carry the cameras. We would concentrate on mollymawks and rockhoppers here, and let the gentoos wait until we got back to Stanley. But Jack told us that the most spectacular colony on the island was the gentoo colony near the Virgin Hotel; too far to walk, but we could ride out.

Gentoos trumpeting; the young seem unimpressed

On the western side, Rookery Hill sloped gradually at first into a circular patch of gray—another rockhopper colony. Beyond that it dropped straight into the sea, except for one slender neck of land that reached out to a great, towering mass of craggy rocks—Landsend, the wildest spot on the island, inhabited only by seals.

Supper was on the table when we got home—cold lamb, cold gosling, homemade bread. I went with Agnes to the store to get some sugar. The building was bursting with cases, boxes, bottles, and tins. In one glance I saw flour, stationery, liver salts, rubber boots, and raisins.

After supper the children disappeared with Jacob for a romp in his quarters; Agnes fussed with a Tilley lamp, as balky as the Cawkells' heater; and Grandpa and I dried dishes for Hazel. She was just sixteen years old and had come from Stanley three years before and was one of the family.

When the children returned, Jack said to Raymond, "Do you know what I'm going to do now?"

"Sure, put your teeth to bed," said his son.

Jack rose and went to the door. With a low bow he bade us all goodnight.

The youngsters undressed before the fire. Snug in their flannel nightgowns, they kissed us all, said a solemn goodnight, and scurried through the cold passage and up the stairs to their feather beds. Grandpa hobbled off to his room, and we lingered with Agnes a few minutes. I was almost afraid to leave—as if this were all a dream and would vanish before morning.

New Island seemed full of possibilities. We made plans for sailing, for riding, for taking pictures—birds, boats, horses, sheep, skuas, Landsend, cats, the Virgin Hotel, the fabulous bird colony on the cliffs. A peace folded about us that night, a security I had not felt in months. New Island was the whole world. Everything else seemed very far away.

Agnes woke us at seven the next morning, bringing us tea. I enjoyed mine, but Sewall took a dim view of early tea and those who indulged in it. I would have to explain this to Agnes.

The sky was sullen and the island darkened by a misty rain; but the kitchen was bright and cheerful when we went down to breakfast at eight. Each member of the family greeted us, and the children kissed us. They were all busy planning their day. Grandpa suggested we all ride up the hill to shoot a few geese, but Jacob reminded him that there were camp skins to be clipped. Jack said no shearing until next week; the holidays would not be over until after New Year's. He and Jacob had some mysterious plan of their own.

Agnes glanced at the clock, dashed into the living room and turned on the wireless. A cheery voice said: "Stanley calling New Island. Stanley calling New Island. Come in New Island. Over."

"New Island answering Stanley. Receiving you loud and clear."

The plane had not made it back and was still at Fox Bay. Agnes arranged for Jack to talk to the manager of Beaver Island at two-thirty; then, with a "Cheerio, over and out," she snapped off the set and carried the heavy wet battery to the window sill in the dining room where she fastened wires to the terminals. An east wind was blowing and the little windmill between the house and the store was turning; it provided the power for recharging the battery.

After breakfast—porridge, bacon, penguin eggs, bread, and tea—Sewall and I set out in the cold mist to explore the shores of Tigre Bay and the small tidal island. The path was littered with the wings of firebirds that had been killed in the night. We walked beyond the jetty to the sand bar, where seven black and white oystercatchers pattered about on the hard wet sand. Approaching the small island we heard a great crashing and tramping in the grass.

"Sea lions," I cried, jumping back.

Two black and white pigs emerged blinking from the tussock.

Several jackass penguins lumbered in from the sea; they were annoyed when we stood between them and the tussock for which they were heading. Off shore we saw the hulk of a half-submerged ship. Jack told us later that it was a coal ship that had broken from its moorings in South Harbour years earlier—before the whaling station moved to South Georgia. They were waiting for her to break up—there was a fortune in coal in her hold.

We left the island and followed the shore line to South Harbour. Logger ducks, a pair about every thirty yards, kept up a constant complaint. Above us the gray slopes were honeycombed with burrows. The larger ones belonged to jackass penguins; but most of them, much smaller, were firebird burrows.

Sewall was excited. New Island was one of the few places in the world where firebirds have actually been found nesting. Little was known about them. Their eggs, one to a burrow, had been described by ornithologists, but, as far as he knew, no one had ever described their young.

He set to work to find a chick. Rolling up a sleeve and brushing away the soft, peaty soil at the burrow entrance, he plunged his arm in almost to the shoulder, and drew out a bird. "This one's still incubating an egg." The bird seemed dazed by daylight. As Sewall stroked its soft plumage and spread one long, slender wing, it struggled a little but made no sound. When he put it down it scurried back into the burrow. In the next one he found a chick, an animated fluffy ball like a gray powder puff. Only a tiny black bill identified it as a bird, for the long down hid even its eyes and feet.

"Looks like the Leach's petrel chicks I used to find on islands off the coast of Maine," he said. "This poor fellow has simply got to be collected. There's probably not a firebird chick in any museum anywhere." I shuddered as he deftly squeezed the bird until it lay limp in his hand, telling myself it was for the sake of science. He slipped it into a paper cone to keep the down from being mussed.

Walking overland toward the settlement we came on a family of red-breasted troupials in a tangle of gorse. There were two adults and three young, and they acted so much like meadowlarks that it seemed as though they had been dipped in the wrong dye pot. They searched for insects in the grass and lit on the swaying gorse, flaunting their flaming breasts. Then they moved out of the gorse to an area where cows had recently been pastured and methodically flipped each cow paddy with their bills, snapping up insects from underneath.

Back at the house I went upstairs to tidy up for dinner. The water pitcher was empty, and I took it down to Hazel, who showed me how to fill it from the tap in a great wooden tank outside the scullery door. Agnes explained that there was often a shortage. New Island was a mass of rock overlaid by porous crumbly soil; it was impossible to dig wells, and the water supply came from a series of tanks that collected rain water from the corrugated metal roofs of the houses and outbuildings. In the summer the rainfall consisted only of squalls, and just now there was little water to spare.

"Take all you need," she said, "but no extra. We all have to be careful."

"Got just the spot to build a reservoir on the side of Old Vic," Jack said at dinner. "Then we'll have plenty of water running right into the new house."

"New house!" I said. "This is a wonderful house."

"The new house is all ordered," Agnes said as calmly as though she picked up a catalogue and ordered a house every other day.

"It will probably be up within a year. I'll be glad to be out of this place with all its dust."

I looked at the windows set in twenty-inch-thick stone walls. "It may be old, but it's snug. How old is it?"

Jack did not know; he did not know who had built it—perhaps the sealers and whalers, for whom New Island was once a convenient stopping place. The Spanish, French, and Scandinavians had been there, and of course, the Yankees.

My imagination leaped at this. I knew that both my grandfather and great-grandfather had sailed around the Horn and stopped at the Falkland Islands. I had leafed through old records at Stanley looking for some mention of their ships. Perhaps they had not gone to Stanley at all; perhaps they had put in at New Island, anchored in Tigre Bay, looked up at Victoria Mountain.

"Jack," I pleaded, "don't tear down this beautiful house."

"I'll leave the original part anyway," he promised. "As near as I can figure the first house was the dining room, kitchen, and the two bedrooms above. That's why there's a separate staircase to your room."

"You should have seen the enormous fireplaces we tore out in the kitchen and sitting room," Agnes said. "There were ovens built right in the sides."

After dinner Agnes brought out blueprints of the new house. It was to be of wood covered with metal, the most sensible construction for the climate. It would be all on one floor with four bedrooms.

There was to be a conservatory across the front. Grandma Davis in Stanley was already raising plants for it. The drapes and linoleum had been ordered from England; it would take seven months to get them. As soon as the stonemasons could come and lay the foundation, the new house would arrive, with a brace of carpenters who would stay on New Island until the house was completed.

Jack insisted that we take a walk, and we started down the track to the head of the bay. Raymond, running beside Sewall, said, "Dad and Jacob swept out the pigs' fattening house this morning."

"You weren't suppose to tell," Jack said. "It's a surprise."

Just before us, above the door of a small weather-worn building was a large sign, "Pettingill's Parlour." Jack and Jacob had cleaned out the pigs' fattening house, which was unused at this season; it was spotless and the brisk breeze had removed all trace of odor. This was to be Sewall's laboratory. Delighted, he moved right in with his bottles, cotton, and scalpels, and began to skin the firebird chick, with Jack watching. He and the shepherds became fascinated by Sewall's museum skins, and from then on saw to it he always had a backlog of specimens to work on. Death was all around us. I became hardened to the mutilated bodies of firebirds in the front garden, the carcasses of turkey vultures and skuas shot by the shepherds, and the empty penguin skins tossed up on the beach. Sewall had plenty of material without firing a single shot. When a very dead logger duck was found in the sand, too far gone to preserve for its skin, he threw it on the beach, where the chickens picked it clean. The skeleton was just what was needed by a student at the University of Michigan.

The next morning Sewall was up early and off to his Parlour. He was hardly out of the house before Agnes appeared with tea.

"You didn't say you didn't want it," she said when I insisted that I didn't want to be treated as company. She then agreed to let me help her with work when I had time.

The wireless that morning brought Sewall and me a special message from the Cawkells: "Congratulations on coming of age. The next will be silver." We did not explain its meaning to the Davises, and they did not inquire. But later at dinner, when Hazel served a rich fruit cake for dessert, Jack said, "What is this I've found in my pudding?" and drew from his lips two ten-shilling notes, which he inspected with an air of surprise. The children were wide-eyed. Jack presented the notes to me, saying, "Please accept these in honor of the day."

"You guessed?" I said. "From the wireless message?"

"We didn't think either of you was celebrating your twenty-first birthday," Agnes said. "Is it a wedding anniversary?"

The youngsters brought more presents—two white china tea plates embossed with the seal of the Falkland Islands. "You may take them home," Helen assured me solemnly.

Sewall and I set out for the cliffs after breakfast. The skies were sunny, but the wind, only a mild breeze in the settlement, swooped down on us once we were on the flat. The cameras grew heavier, and we decided it would be safe to leave them there at noon, but not overnight because of the dampness.

We had already selected a site in the rockhopper colony where we could take detailed pictures of birds on their nests. There was plenty of activity. The rockhopper nests each had eggs or one small chick. Skuas circled constantly overhead; and mollymawks glided about, hardly moving their wings. Shags, returning from fishing, streamed by in long lines.

We set up the cameras amid a great din. Not all the birds were yammering, we soon realized, and none of them was yammering at us. The adults around us sat quietly on their nests. The noise was made by the birds that were coming up the gully from the sea. Clean from their swim, they had to run or hop between the nesting birds, which reached out to nip them. Rockhoppers had an easier time running the gauntlet than the gentoos we had seen; they could move faster, and got fewer jabs in the ribs; but the rockhoppers jabbed more viciously. Few homecoming birds ever reached their nests without being assailed several times; some of them got confused, forgot the location of their nests, and darted about aimlessly, receiving some fearful pinches.

These rockhoppers are not necessarily angry—they do this all the time

When they arrived safely at their nests there was great rejoicing. The mate, alone for some time—perhaps for several days— stretched its neck skyward and, shaking its head wildly back and forth, let out a series of ear-piercing cackles. The newcomer, after first bowing low, imitated its mate's performance. This act was repeated again and again until the neighbors all around the reunited pair joined in to produce an outburst of cacophonous cries. With the birds returning all day in a steady stream, there was never a quiet moment; by late afternoon, when they would come in full force, it would be deafening.

The skuas grew bolder and flew lower, and one lighted on a high rock near us. Handsome in flight, it looked like an ugly gull on the ground, although it is not a gull, but closely related to the jaegers. Skuas or no skuas, the penguins never left their nests unguarded. The birds stuck to their nests so tenaciously that in order to photograph a small chick by itself Sewall had to push the adult away. It returned immediately to its chick; finally Sewall carried an especially plump chick to an open area for a portrait. The adult bird, not missing the chick, moved back to its nest and sat quietly, and Sewall focused on the downy youngster and pressed the button. Before I knew what was happening the skua swooped down, picked up the baby, carried it to the high rock, and swallowed it in one gulp.

"Why didn't you scare it away?" Sewall asked. I was too upset to explain. Thereafter when we photographed baby penguins I hovered over them waving a skua stick above my head.

We continued to photograph in the afternoon, even though the weather was abominable and the squalls came so fast that there was hardly time between them to uncover the cameras. We went home and were relaxing by the fire with Jack and Grandpa when Agnes and the children, who had been fishing from the beach at Ship Harbour, returned.

"Come and see what we caught," Raymond called. We rushed out to view the catch—eight huge mullet, each more than two feet long.

From the wash house door Agnes called, "Want to help me clean these for supper?" Thinking that all fishermen should clean their own catch, and never having been a fisherman myself, I ignored this. Then I realized with horror that Agnes was looking at me. I turned desperately to Sewall, who had a way of being very busy at such times. He grinned over his shoulder as he hurried to his Parlour. I thought of begging off until I recalled that I had promised that morning to help Agnes with the work whenever I could.

"Sure," I said lamely, "but I never cleaned a mullet."

"I guess all fish are alike," she said.

In the wash house I picked up a wicked-looking knife, lifted a mullet, and watching Agnes's every move, cut off the head, slit the belly, ripped out the guts, and tossed it in a tub. After the fourth fish, I felt I was performing like a master. Disposing of the offal was easy enough: the cats lined up for a feast at the wash house door, and I watched them stuff themselves until they bulged. At least the firebirds will be safe tonight, I thought; but my own appetite was gone, and did not return until the fish appeared on the table, baked in a vinegar sauce.

That evening someone remembered it was New Year's Eve, and Jack turned on the radio. The special program, short-waved from London to the colonies, was so dull that we turned it off to save the batteries for the Voice of America at midnight.

"We used to have exciting programs from the States—lots of good popular music," Agnes said. "Lately it's just been dull lectures."

• "It will be exciting tonight," I assured her. "They'll broadcast from Times Square. There'll be sounds of the holiday crowd, and bells, and everybody will sing 'Auld Lang Syne.'"

I have never been so wrong. The Voice of America wasn't celebrating New Year's Eve. The broadcast consisted of a lecture in monotone on recent developments in education.

There was a bustle in the house the next morning. Promptly at eight we sat down to breakfast of mutton chops. The horses, already saddled, stood by the peat-shed gate. Old Stump waited impatiently by the front door. The gathering of the sheep was about to begin.

Jack mounted his horse Chico, and sat relaxed in the saddle. Tony Felton and Bob Keddle, followed by their dogs, rode up the track. Jacob, in sailor blouse, bombaches, and a blue beret stroked his beard and patted his favorite horse Tony. They all rode away toward the north end to bring in the sheep for shearing; by noon they would have a thousand.

The weather was too poor for photography on the cliffs, and Sewall and I spent most of the morning scrambling over the rocks in the gully, searching for the perfect place from which to photográph the landing rockhoppers. Few penguins came in at this time of day, but there were plenty of birds on the rocks close to the water. Some were snoozing, some were swimming in small tidal pools, rolling over, porpoising, and diving; others were dallying under the little streams that dribbled over the face of the cliff. They took turns standing under one small waterfall to enjoy a shower bath and a drink of fresh water. There was a stream of fresh water in every rockhopper colony we visited.

We watched the penguins going to sea. Although they landed on only one rock, they left from several places. Some walked cautiously down a smooth ledge and waited for the waves to sweep them seaward; most of them, however, climbed in groups up a broken ledge that extended out and dropped about six feet to the water, advanced to the edge, peeked over, backed up, went forward again, and finally jumped in feet first. When one jumped, most of the group followed, or were pushed. If they could have held their beaks with their flippers, they would have looked just like kids in the old swimming hole. But there were some that walked to the edge, took one look, turned around, hopped back to the slanting ledge, and waded in.

The sun came out at noon and we hurried back to the settlement in time to photograph the sheep coming in. With cameras ready to grind, we stood on the hill behind the killing shed when a stream of sheep, guided by dogs and shepherds walking beside their horses, literally flowed over the side of the mountain and poured down onto the flat. While the dogs corralled the animals into a tight little circle, the men opened the paddock gates. Then the dogs, barking happily, forced the sheep, laboring under their heavy burden of wool, from one paddock to another until they were safe in the rough sheep pasture, where they would remain until they were sheared.

The whole settlement had turned out to greet the shepherds. Tony Felton and Bob Keddle lifted their small youngsters up on their horses for a ride to the gearing shed. Helen rode Tony, and Raymond sat proudly on Chico.

After dinner Agnes said, "It's time you had a ride, Ellie." I had been dreading this. I looked at Sewall; he pointed to his arm smugly; I could see he would be no more help with horses than he had been with fish.

"Horses never like me," I said faintly. "I'm afraid and they know it."

Undaunted, Agnes rounded up Pela and Tony and led them to the shearing shed. "Meet me at the Parlour in ten minutes," she said as she passed the house.

When I met her with Tony by the Parlour, I tried to pat him. He was unimpressed. As Agnes adjusted the stirrups she gave me a brief outline of his background that failed to reassure me: "He used to be a race horse. I bought him for two shillings from his owner, who was about to shoot him. He's old, but he's still pretty good."

Patiently she helped me mount. The western saddle with its sheepskin cover was comfortable enough. Tony stood very still; Pela danced about, anxious to be off.

"Come on," said Agnes, swinging into her saddle. "Oh, for heaven's sake, tighten the rein and let go the horn. Never hold the saddle horn."

Tense as a piano wire, I took a deep breath and obeyed. Tony began to jog after Pela. When I slackened the reins, he stopped. Finally I caught on: he was trained that way. I pulled in the reins and gave him several whacks on the flank and he was off again. I thought it was the terrain that was bumpy, but Jack told me later that little Tony could give the roughest ride of all the New Island horses when he felt like it.

Letting the horses pick the way through the white grass and diddle-dee, dodging penguin burrows and rocky outcrops, we rode to the ridge above Ship Harbour. There I dismounted and found my legs were like rubber. Agnes laughed and told me to take a few steps, and I recovered. Mounting again, we rode on, following the sheep paths above the sea. Everything went well. I was beginning to enjoy it when we came around the mountain and Tony and Pela spotted the settlement on the far side of the bay. Laying their ears back, they both headed straight down the mountain as fast as they could go. I managed to hang on somehow. As we passed the Parlour at a gallop I caught a glimpse of Sewall's shocked face.

"It's wonderful!" I called. I pulled on the reins to stop the horse. He only went faster until he reached the gearing shed where he stopped abruptly of his own accord.

"It's simply wonderful," I told Agnes as we dismounted.

"Of course it is," she said casually, as if she had known all along I would like it.

Later that afternoon, Sewall and I went to the rockhopper colony where penguins were landing by the hundreds; but a wild hail storm drove us home. The family was listening to the weekly broadcast from Stanley to the camp. Besides news for the farmers, social notes, hospital notes, and news from travelers, there were personal messages. Children who had birthdays coming within the week were congratulated and told where to look for presents— in the cupboard off the passage or under the cushions of the sitting-room sofa. The next trip of the *Fitzroy* around the camp was announced for April, two months away, and it was suggested that orders for supplies be placed as soon as possible. The *Gambler* was off for the Sea Lions and the *Philomel* was due to leave any day for Beaver Island. Agnes made a note to send a message to Grandma Davis to pick up ten yards of elastic to put on the *Philomel,* which was sure to stop at New Island, and to talk to Dr. Slessor on the wireless about sending the plane for Mally to take her to Stanley for her confinement.

After supper Jack asked us to come out to watch sheep being put in the shearing shed. They would have dried out enough after the hailstorm. Sheep must be dry when sheared, for moisture in the bale will rot the wool. In a climate like the Falklands, it is quite a trick to have the shearing shed full of dry sheep, but not too full. The animals must be dry; the work must not stop for a moment; yet the sheep cannot be kept in the shed without food and water for any length of time.

When we came out of the cozy house into the bitter cold, Old Stump rose from his place by the doorstep. Jacob patted his head, and he wriggled with pleasure.

"As long as there are sheep in the rough sheep pasture, Old Stump never leaves the settlement," Jack said. "He's afraid he'll miss the fun of putting them in the shed."

Old Stump raced ahead of us down the track. I don't know whether Old Stump belonged to Jack or to Jacob; it was Jacob who gave the commands with whistles. Driving sheep into the pens was Old Stump's finest accomplishment and he needed no other dogs to help him. With precision and finesse he rounded up a flock of sheep—just enough for one day's shearing—and drove them into an outside pen; Jack opened another gate and, nipping gently at their heels, the dog urged the bewildered animals down a ramp and into the shed, where there was a series of smaller pens. Amid scampering and bleating in clouds of dust, we followed the sheep inside and helped fasten the pens. The animals stared at us dumbly; with all the curly wool around their faces they looked like old ladies just returned from a frizzing at the beauty parlor.

On Saturday morning the weather was so bad that Sewall went to his Parlour, and I seized the opportunity to try out Agnes's spinning wheel. I carried it to the sitting room; Hazel spread an old sheet under it to catch the dust; and Grandpa clipped a few handfuls of wool from the camp skins that hung over the fence by the corner of the house.

With everybody gathered around giving directions, Agnes sat down at the wheel. After combing the wool to remove bits of diddle-dee and straighten the fibers, she twisted it between her fingers to make a short length of yarn, passed it through some holes, and tied it to a spool. Then with a batch of wool in her right hand and her left hand free to draw out the fibers, she pressed the foot treadle. The yarn knotted and broke. She tried again with the same result. She admitted she didn't like to spin and seemed to have forgotten the little she had learned. We tightened strings here and loosened knobs there. Gradually she managed to spin a few feet without breaking the thread.

"Maybe we should wash it first?" I said, looking at my hands, black from combing the wool.

"You never wash it first. That I do know," Agnes said. "The grease makes the fibers stick together. That's lanolin on your hands. Wonderful for them. The shepherds' hands get soft as babies' during shearing."

I took over, and with Helen at my feet combing wool and Raymond pressing the treadle, we made the wheel really whirl, and the wool, knotty and bumpy and irregular though it was, wound onto the spool. I kept on until I had one whole spool of what I thought was yarn. When I proudly displayed it, Agnes took me down by informing me that the most difficult part was yet to come. I must spin another spool and twist the two strands together to make proper yarn. I persisted in spinning whenever the weather kept us indoors and after I had two spools of wool, Agnes and I put the strands together. At last we had a big sticky ball of gray, greasy, lumpy yarn. Recalling the stunning sweaters knitted from rough wool by the Indians of the Canadian Northwest, I decided to make a pair of mittens, small ones, for Helen. Agnes was dubious, but I was stubborn, and eventually I finished them.

That morning Mally and Winnie came over with market baskets and milk pails. It was Saturday, time for marketing, and Agnes took care of the needs of the shepherds' wives at the store while Hazel filled their pails with milk. Mally was very pregnant; I hoped the plane that Agnes had asked for by wireless would not be long in coming.

There was plenty of milk. Bob Keddle milked every morning in a cow shed; once a day was enough, for the feed was sparse on New Island. The Davis family's milk was scalded in large pans on the kitchen stove, then placed outdoors in a "milk safe," a screened box on four legs, for three days before it was skimmed —"fresh milk was bad." The cream was used for butter, the milk for tea and cereal.

The Davises, in addition to providing each shepherd's family with a house, supplied all their milk, mutton, and peat. They sold them other supplies at Stanley prices, with no charge for freight; all the men's meals, when they worked outside the settlement, were prepared by Agnes. The men had regular hours with Saturday afternoons and Sundays off. All medical services were provided by the government, even the plane to take Mally to the hospital. Their pay was £19, or about $54 a month; with all the extras, it was adequate.

When the rain stopped, Agnes and I braced ourselves against the wind that swept down from the mountain and went out to the garden to gather new potatoes. When I asked for a fork to dig them, Agnes said, "You don't *dig* new potatoes, you scratch for them." I learned on bended knee how to gather new potatoes without disturbing the plant, how to run my fingers carefully through the soil and detach the smooth lumps from the roots. I became so skillful as the summer went on that Agnes trusted me to go alone to the garden.

After dinner Sewall and I walked out to the colony. It was glorious on the cliffs; the storm had churned up high waves that

crashed like thunder on the rocks. In the smooth troughs the
water was blue-green, the same color we had seen as we approached the island by plane. We took photographs of the sea
in tumult, the mollymawks sailing in the fierce wind, the shags
flying home in unbroken ranks. We wanted to take pictures of
the rockhoppers landing in the crashing surf, but all the rocks
in the gully were streaming with water and we could not find
a safe place for the cameras or ourselves.

When we came back to the settlement in the late afternoon,
chilled and wet, Agnes hailed us from the door of the wash
house. I stepped into the large, warm room where Agnes was
pushing tubs and racks around, sorting clothes in piles, and
occasionally tossing lumps of peat into a stone fireplace below
a massive water tank, called the "copper." She was getting ready
for Saturday night baths. While I helped her by scrubbing out
the enormous tub in which I had cleaned the mullet I asked if
there was enough water for baths.

"Yes, if we all go easy. Anyhow, it's Saturday night and we
all *have* to have baths." She hesitated. "Do you and Sewall want
baths here?"

I had been as careful as possible of water, limiting our ablutions
and simple laundry to the contents of the pitcher which I filled
once a day. Having a real bath had not occurred to me. In fact
baths in Stanley had been such a torment that I was happy to
forget about them.

"There is nothing in the world I would rather have right now
than a hot bath in a warm room," I said.

She smiled and looked relieved. "Some of our guests have
thought they were too good to take baths in the wash house,"
she said. "I'll just pop the children in first."

The children were popped into the tub and scrubbed, hair and
all, while they laughed and played and dashed us with soapsuds.
Then they were dressed in clean, freshly ironed clothes, Raymond
in gray flannel shorts, starched white shirt, and green sweater;
Helen in a tartan skirt, fluffy white blouse, and red jumper.
I thought of my own limited wardrobe; I could only wear a
different blouse with the same tired gray skirt. I hoped Agnes
would not be insulted when she realized, as she would in four
weeks, how few dress-up clothes I'd brought. Although she was

a shepherd's daughter and had spent nearly all her thirty-five years in the West, she was intelligent and keen; she knew exactly how everything should be done on a well-run farm, and nothing in her household was ever slipshod. That night she wore a becoming black dress for supper.

It was nearly dark when Sewall and I, bath towels in hand, went to the wash house. The room was hot. Clouds of steam from the copper enveloped us, and droplets caught in the cobwebs of the rafters above and shone like diamonds in the firelight.

As I was dipping hot water from the copper to the tub I had an idea. When Sewall stepped into the tub, I snatched the precious orlon underwear he had taken off, the underwear he guarded with awful threats and refused to be separated from and sometimes even slept in. I tossed it into the water at one end of the long tub, grabbed a scrub board, and went at it.

"What on earth are you doing?" he asked peering through the steam and the dim light at me, wrapped in a bath towel, on my knees.

"Just rinsing out a few things," I said, as offhand as if I always did laundry in this informal way.

"My God! It's my underwear," he shouted. "You've got it all wet!"

With that we collapsed into a fit of laughter. If we woke Jacob in his room next door, he thought nothing of it. Everyone laughed at everything on New Island.

As I looked back over the week that Saturday night, I had a feeling of satisfaction. I had learned to clean fish, spin, ride horseback, and scratch for potatoes. There seemed to be no end to the experiences New Island had to offer.

On Monday, January 4, the holidays were over. Jack and Jacob left for the shearing shed, Agnes disappeared in the direction of the wash house, Hazel and the children retired for lessons in the sitting room, and Grandpa sat alone in his armchair in the kitchen.

Jack and Agnes were as firm about the children's lessons as about meals and working hours; in spite of the distractions of New Island, the children began school at nine and ended at three, with time out for smoko and dinner.

Hazel had finished her formal education in Stanley when she

completed the eighth grade. She was totally unaware of any rules of pedagogy, yet I marveled at the way she managed Helen and Raymond. They resisted her drilling at times, but she kept them hard at it—reading, writing, spelling, and simple arithmetic. Strangely enough her rigid discipline never seemed to frustrate or inhibit them. They were extraordinarily sweet, good-tempered children.

For a few weeks each year Hazel's job was taken over by one of Edwin Cawkell's traveling teachers. Actually he did little more than check on the youngsters' progress and outline future work. The burden of their education rested on the sixteen-year-old girl. Very shortly little Sonja Felton would be five and ready to join Hazel's class.

Edwin approved the Davises' views on education. I recalled his despair when he tried to arrange for the instruction of other children in remote areas where many of the parents were unable or unwilling to teach them even the most elementary things, and traveling teachers were not always "made welcome." Some farmers resisted the whole idea. "If we educate them all," one of them said to Edwin, "they'll spend their winter evenings reading instead of making horse gear."

Sewall and I went to work too. On our way to the colony we spotted a gray-brown hump through the mist and rain.

"Sheep down!"

We pulled and tugged at the poor frightened animal until we got it to its feet. From that time on Jack left the shepherding of the flat to us, since we passed over it twice a day. Later we also kept a sharp lookout for lambs in the ditches.

This day we photographed the feeding of the penguin babies. After a bird returned from the sea and greeted its mate effusively, it responded to the wiggles and pecks of the offspring by bending over and regurgitating a mass of shrimps into its open, upraised mouth. The parent then rested a bit, repeated the process, rested again, and fed the chick again until it was so stuffed it couldn't walk even if it wanted to. Relaxed in torpor, it couldn't even move.

We selected ten nests close together, nine with one baby, one with an egg, and each guarded by an adult. With waterproof paint, the quick-drying kind used for painting toy airplanes, we marked each adult and chick on the back with a huge number in bright yellow.

"We'll come back tonight and number any mates that come in from the sea," Sewall said. "The bill of the male is just a little bit thicker and heavier than the female's, so when we see the two birds together we should be able to distinguish the sexes."

Then we went to work on the king shags, the colony within the colony of rockhopper penguins. The wind was bitterly cold, but the sky remained clear and blue—the first really good photographic conditions in nearly a week.

King shags on their nests

The shags' nests, in neat rows and very close together, were big humps of matted tussock and seaweed with only a slight indentation in the top for the eggs or the young. The greeting ceremony of these birds was quiet compared to their boisterous penguin neighbors, but it was far more ludicrous. With their great pink feet outspread against the stiff wind, the birds dropped down on the rims of their nests with awkward plops, just beside their mates. Both birds then stretched their necks high and bowed, with their heads and necks swaying back and forth in unison. After they had done this a few times, they twisted their necks so that each could nibble at the other's head and throat. There was no hurry about it. The nibbling went on as long as there were two birds on the nest.

Some nests had eggs; in others there were small young. As soon as we had chosen a vantage point and the slight confusion we had caused subsided, we noticed a number of dolphin gulls fly down and form a ring around the colony. They stood quietly, rising occasionally to circle over the shags. When they came too close, the shags waggled their necks menacingly and uttered low guttural sounds.

I pushed a shag off its nest to get a picture of the eggs. The bird struggled back onto it at once, and I shoved it off again. Instantly a dolphin gull dropped down to the nest and flew away with an egg in its bill. Chagrined at having been caught unawares, I let the poor shag return to its one remaining egg.

"Do that again," Sewall said. "I must have a picture of it. Get an egg from another nest and put it in this nest and push the shag off."

I did, and he focused the camera on it; but before he had time to push the button the egg was gone. Eventually we learned how to get pictures of the gulls stealing eggs. When I forced the shag from its nest, I held my hands cupped over its eggs until I heard the camera running. Every time I raised my hands, one of the gulls—there were always several hovering overhead—would swoop down with incredible speed and help itself to an egg.

In the afternoon we photographed the rockhoppers coming up the gully. Sewall realized now that penguins, not water, had scratched the rocks, and he took close-up pictures of their strong pink feet and sharp claws scarring them still deeper. I tried counting the birds as they bobbed past in single file. It was like counting the cars on a fast freight. I told Sewall that I had counted eighty-five a minute—better than one per second—but he insisted it couldn't be true.

"That's only five thousand birds an hour," I said. "You estimated, didn't you, that there are forty thousand penguins on the cliffs? Well, there are only two paths. If half the birds come up once a day, most of them during the afternoon rush hour, there could be at least eighty-five a minute." Of course we did not know how often one bird might go to sea. Whatever the number, it was startling.

We stayed late enough that evening to catch some of the mates on our ten marked nests. These birds had smaller bills, so we knew they were females; we numbered them with red paint. When we checked again the next day, all the males were at home, each standing by its chick, and the females were all away. It was evident that the females fished all day and returned to their families only at night.

When we got back to the house for supper, we found Agnes on pins and needles because the plane had not come for Mally. She had a medical kit, furnished by the government and kept under lock and key. With that, plus wireless instructions from Dr. Slessor, she was supposed to be able to cope with any emergency until a doctor could fly out or the patient could be taken to the hospital in Stanley. I was wondering how much she really could do when she turned to me. "What do you know about such things, Ellie?" she asked.

"Nothing," I replied firmly. "If you have me in mind as a midwife, please forget it right now. I'll carry the peat and boil the water. You always boil water."

She asked Sewall next. He turned pale when she suggested that the "Dr." in front of his name ought to be good for something besides skinning birds.

"Now, not to worry," Jacob said soothingly. He raised his knife and carved the lamb with the skill of a surgeon. "Just keep calm and leave everything to me. I've got a pair of tongs and a lasso put aside for just such an emergency."

We spent one morning photographing mollymawks—handsome, stupid albatrosses which, if their one egg was removed from the nest, continued to sit there throughout the nesting season, not realizing the loss and apparently not caring. The mollies were marvels of grace in the air, but slow and awkward on land and so dependent on the wind that they could be earthbound in a calm. New Island was an ideal habitat for them because of the incessant strong winds.

As we watched them soaring and circling over the colony we tried to guess where each bird would light. Their feet dropped down and the long slim wings folded slowly as they descended into the wind to land near nest and mate. Their nests were far apart, mud chimneys built at random among the close nests of the shags and rockhoppers. Many times a molly landed some distance from home and had to plod through the muddy colony to reach it. I never understood how they kept their white plumage so immaculate; they were always the best-groomed birds in the colony.

They never hurried. Once a pair was reunited on their nest, the "dance" of the albatross began. First the partners bowed; then the homecoming bird took a step, bowed, took another, and bowed, while the bird on the nest did the same. Then they bowed again in unison. This was repeated time after time with great deliberation. While the little rockhoppers fussed and cackled near by, and the king shags twisted their necks and bobbed their heads, the great black and white mollies, oblivious of their frenetic neighbors, continued dancing, stopping now and then to preen as a variation. When the dance was finally over, the nibbling began; they scratched and tickled each other for hours, sometimes opening their mouth in a soundless gape.

When the dancing and nibbling were over, the albatross that had been guarding the nest stepped down slowly and the home-comer, after a pause, stepped up. The bird that had been relieved was in no hurry to get away even though it might have been on the nest for several days. There was more dancing and nibbling before it lumbered across the colony to the edge of the cliffs where it waited patiently for just the right gust of wind. When a strong updraft came from the sea, the albatross, with complete detachment, unfolded its great wings and floated away.

The mollies acknowledged my presence by turning on their nests so that they were always facing me; but still I felt as if I were not there as far as they were concerned. They stared at me vacantly down their long bills. They must have regarded me as just one more penguin, a bit oversized, perhaps, but none-theless just another bird.

When we went home to dinner, Jack had a present for me— the skin of the lamb we had eaten our first day on New Island. It was dirty and greasy and clots of blood and fat still clung to the underside.

"All you have to do is wash it twice—whenever Agnes heats the copper," Jack said. "Then we'll show you how to rub it with a brick."

I washed it twice and it emerged from the second bath white and fluffy. In spare moments I rubbed it with an old brick.

Grandpa rubbed, Raymond rubbed, in fact almost everyone had a go at it. Sometimes I thought it would be easier if I chewed it, as Eskimo women chew sealskins; but gradually the skin became soft and pliable.

We had a luckless afternoon on the cliffs. One roll of still film was spoiled, and when I tried to renew the numbers on the penguins I spilled most of the yellow paint. Wild squalls drove us home tired and dejected.

As we sat in the kitchen waiting for supper, Agnes must have sensed that we were weary and disheartened by the weather. She took a volume from among her cookbooks and handed it to Sewall saying, "Ever hear of these? By Robert W. Service. Someone left it here."

Sewall opened the book and smiled as he came on the familiar lines:

"There are strange things done in the midnight sun
By the men who moil for gold."

He read on in melodramatic tones how "Sam McGee was from Tennessee—was always cold, but the land of gold seemed to hold him like a spell." By the time Sam McGee was in the furnace the children were bug-eyed. Agnes took the book and declaimed, "A bunch of the boys were whooping it up in the Malamute saloon. . . ."

We sat down to supper with more sourdough verses and then turned to lines from other poets memorized long ago—Tennyson, Longfellow, and Shakespeare. As Hazel poured the last cup of tea Sewall was reciting Poe's *Raven*, the rest of us accompanying him with appropriate gestures.

As for the weariness, it was forgotten, as it usually was on New Island. By the light of the candle I wrote in my journal: "These days on New Island are heavenly. Except for the heavy cameras, everything is such fun."

The next morning I could tell from the way the *Penguin* and the *Overseas* tossed and pulled at their moorings in the turbulent gray harbor that we could not go to the colony. I went down to the wool shed at smoko time to take Jacob his tea; then, perched on the gate of the clipping pen, I watched Tony, the champion shearer. Seated on a stool, he placed the sheep beside him on its behind and put his arm cosily about its neck. Beginning from the mid-ventral line and working from front to back, he clipped off the fleece as though he were peeling off an overcoat. The sheet of wool fell to the floor in one piece. It took less than ten minutes.

The larger farms used mechanical shearers; on New Island the sheep were still clipped by hand with what looked like grass-trimming shears. Electric clippers cut the wool too close for the climate, was Jack's explanation (that, and the fact that New Island had no electricity). "A sudden cold spell, and you lose a lot of animals. I don't get quite so much wool, but I have something left to grow more on."

Jacob picked up Tony's fleece and carried it to a long table. There he tore off the inferior bits and tossed them into a bin. The rest he rolled into a bundle, fastened it with a loop at the neck end, and tossed it into the loft. As he worked he felt the fleece carefully for any sign of coarseness or hair. A sheep that bore scratchy wool went to the killing shed. Jack was proud of the quality of his wool; for several years it had received the highest price of all the Falkland wool on the London market, and he tried to keep up to his standard. The best wool came from yearlings; after that it grew coarser; he never intentionally kept a sheep after the fourth year.

At noon the sun came out and the wind moderated. Agnes asked me to go for a walk, hinting that she wanted to show me something secret. We pushed our way through the overgrown garden in front of the house and followed a steep path that led abruptly to some rocks just above the water. From there we took another trail along the sea toward the head of the harbor, a trail I had never even noticed. Struggling through gorse and veronica that had somehow taken root in the rocky soil, we came to a grassy nook above the path. Ledges overhung it, and the rocks dropped away below. The sun poured in.

"This is my summer resort," Agnes said. "Sometimes I sit here and read or sew and keep an eye on the children on the beach."

There were bright red poppies in the grass, escaped from the garden above. We sat in the sun and Agnes talked to me about the family. When Grandpa, her father, lived alone in Stanley he grew weaker each day. Since he had come to New Island he was better. A shepherd all his life, he had found work again—

clipping wool from the skins of sheep found dead in the camp. For Grandpa every day was fine, and although he suffered from gout and rheumatism, he was always ready to talk about going up the hill to shoot geese.

Jacob Goss was Jack's best friend; he had sailed with Jack and helped him with his boats. When Jack bought New Island four years previously, Jacob gave up his job as a shepherd on a neighboring island and boarded the next *Fitzroy*. Agnes and the children were on the same voyage, bound for their new home.

"Jacob Goss," Agnes called to him, "wherever are you going?"

"To New Island," he said.

Later she said to Jack, "What luck that you could get Jacob."

"I didn't get Jacob," he told her, surprised. "I thought you did."

Jacob admitted that nobody had hired him. He knew Jack needed help on his new farm and he came. For Jacob, New Island was good. His room, warmed by a pot-bellied stove, was bright with pictures of his children, grandchildren, and friends. He was a hero to Helen and Raymond; they rode all over the camp with him, collected penguin eggs, explored the seal caves, and on rare quiet days, paddled in the harbor in the pram.

"Jacob says he will stay five years," Agnes said. "Then he's going back to Stanley for a visit."

It was hard to leave Agnes's sunny nook to face the cold wind on the cliffs. Jack went with us that afternoon. Sewall wanted to take the cameras out on a rocky ledge where sea lions reclined, the best place from which to photograph the landing rockhoppers. Jack was not quite certain it was safe, and we were glad to have his company. We threw a few rocks at the sea lions, and they roared and slipped into the water and never came back. In our desire to get the best possible pictures of penguins landing, we lost a chance to make detailed studies of sea lions. But the penguin pictures would be unusual, and similar views of the sea lions would be ordinary, not to say repulsive. I never saw a sea lion that was not a mass of ugly scars and open sores. They cruised back and forth off shore watching us curiously and occasionally deflecting a stream of land-bound rockhoppers, but we never saw one try to snatch a penguin. We only saw the evidence —penguin skins on the shore.

Our presence on the ledge did not disturb the rockhoppers.

They porpoised toward their rock by the hundreds and sprang from the surf. Some of them made it the first time; others missed, were swept back and had to try again. Each time a few became entangled in the kelp, which held them fast until the next wave lifted them free. They were always exuberant, as if battling the sea were exhilarating.

Sewall shot eleven hundred feet of film and dozens of stills, with Jack acting as handyman, carrying cameras back and forth and continually calling attention to some unusual activity. He was vastly entertained by the "little chaps" coming in from the sea. With all his years in Falkland waters, I doubt if he had ever before observed the landing penguins so closely. He spotted a sheathbill, the first we had seen since Kidney Cove, and I took four still shots of it. Each time I snapped the camera the sheathbill came closer until I could see its homely face and peculiar growth about the base of its bill.

The next time we checked our numbered birds we found a slight variation in their routine. All the males were home guarding the babies. One female was there to spend the day; another female arrived and fed her chick as we watched. Females of two other nests showed up for the first time and we numbered them. The numbers on the back of the poor lonely bird who was still sitting on a dirty egg had to be changed from yellow to red, for the mate that came all fresh and clean from a long time at sea proved to be a male. All the chicks had grown enormously, but so far none had left the nest.

The same day we noticed for the first time some rockhoppers that were just like the nesting birds except that they were slenderer, had brown eyes instead of red, and lacked the yellow plumes over the ears. They seemed unsophisticated, unsure of themselves, standing idly on rocks all around the colony and up and down the edges of the paths. Sewall decided that they must be yearlings with an incipient urge to take part in the nesting activity; but it would be another year before they would be old enough. As the season wore on many more of these subadults appeared.

One afternoon I rode with Agnes to the south end, armed against skuas with a stick tied to my saddle by narrow thongs, "tientas." With Old Stump racing beside us we rode straight across the point to South Harbour and along the beach and slippery rocks. Plots of tussock had been fenced off as a reserve food supply for the sheep, and we entered a plantation so thick the horses could hardly find a trail. Tony and Pela liked tussock too, and bit off huge mouthfuls of it.

We rode up a hill overlooking a sweep of grass where the Davises' cattle grazed, providing them with beef in the winter. Suddenly we were in skua territory. "Quick, Ellie, the stick!" Agnes shrieked. "Put up the stick!"

I fumbled with the tientas. Agnes moved close to me, and Old Stump, who had been sniffing at firebird burrows, came tearing across the camp with skuas in hot pursuit, and took shelter under my horse. Holding the stick high I rode boldly among the skuas, with Old Stump trotting right under Tony.

When we got home and were walking up the track from the gearing shed, Agnes suddenly let out a whoop and ran for the house. She came back carrying a gun and threw herself on the bank between the house and the store. There was a terrific roar, and a huge bird fell from the sky. Agnes dashed up the hill and brought back a dead skua.

"I won't have these near the house, looking at my chickens," she said. "Here's a specimen for Sewall's Parlour."

The weather the next day was dreadful, and we could not photograph penguins. Sewall was worried. "Those birds are growing up—what are we going to do?" But immediately after dinner the clouds lifted and we went to the colony. An inspection of the numbered rockhoppers showed all the chicks on the right nests. For the first time three chicks sat alone with no adults to guard them; they must have been about ten days old. No skuas bothered them. On one nest, the chick guarded by a male was enormous, over half as big as its parent and much larger than any of the chicks that had been left alone.

"Mentally retarded?" I suggested.

"Or burdened with an oversolicitous parent," Sewall said. Actually it might have been the location of the nest—on the edge of the colony and a little apart from the others. It was not as safe. Or possibly the brooding urge of the adult just hadn't run its course.

We concentrated that afternoon on a pair of skuas that occupied a nest on the high rim of the cliff. They nearly went wild when we approached their single downy young one with our sticks held high, diving closer and closer as we looked over the chick, which tried to hide in a few spears of grass beside the nest. There was a ring of baby penguin corpses around the nest; by this time I had seen so much of dead creatures I was no longer shocked or surprised. We retreated a safe distance and took pictures of the adult skuas playing tug of war with penguin remains and feeding bits to the chick.

King shag and young

As if this were not gory enough, we turned to the king shag colony where a couple of skuas were hard at work tearing up a live baby shag that had fallen or been pulled from its nest. It was too late to rescue it. Dolphin gulls walked about looking on but not interfering with the skuas; when the two skuas had wrenched the body apart and each flown away with a mouthful, the gulls closed in for the leavings. The shags merely looked on, not seeming to care.

"Good drama for Disney," Sewall said. He had photographed the whole disgusting scene.

The squalls north and south of us brought masses of cold air over the cliffs, and we headed home, blown down the flat by the wind. When we entered the house, the Davises were listening to the camp news on the wireless.

"We all have to write letters tonight," Agnes said. "The plane is definitely scheduled for tomorrow and it *has* to come."

"The letters won't leave Stanley until the *Fitzroy* sails on January 29," Sewall said, "and we'll be there then."

"You'd better send some tomorrow, just in case . . ." Agnes said. There was no use arguing with her. We all wrote letters.

Saturday was another bad day, but at eight-fifteen the wireless reported fair weather in Stanley; the plane would leave at ten.

Mally was notified. Jack watched the wave-tossed harbor anxiously; Grandpa looked at the sky and shook his head. Raymond was the first to sight the tiny speck above the Colliers. As the plane settled in the harbor, Bob and Jack left the jetty with Mally and young Bob in the bouncy pram. Holding our breath, we watched the men lift and push Mally into the plane and hand the little boy to the pilot, while the plane bobbed in the rough water.

The pilot fought the weather only as far as Fox Bay, where they were stormbound for three days. Mally reached the hospital in Stanley on Tuesday; the baby girl was born just two hours later.

That afternoon Sewall wanted to dig out firebirds from their burrows, and asked Jack for a shovel. He already had specimens of small fluffy chicks; now he wanted large fluffy chicks.

"You don't need a shovel," Jack said. "Take Old Stump. There's nothing he likes better than digging out firebirds."

Old Stump was called and happily set out with Sewall to the

side of the mountain where the firebird burrows were thickest. Stump could indeed dig out baby firebirds, in less than a minute. But he also ate them. Before Sewall could recover a single specimen it was between Stump's jaws and, after a loud crunch, down his throat.

Sewall told him to stop and go home, but Stump was having fun and kept on. Then, alas, Sewall whistled. The dog was beside himself with joy. Forgetting the firebirds he took off in a bee line for the far end of the flat where the ewes and lambs grazed. Methodically he began rounding them up and driving them toward the killing-shed gate. The more frantically Sewall called and whistled, the faster Stump worked. Afraid that some harm might come to the sheep Sewall hurried to the house, calling for help. Jacob, just emerging from his Saturday bath, jumped into his clothes and together they ran to the flat where they met Stump and a large flock of sheep by the killing shed. The dog was waiting for someone to open the gate.

At the sight of Jacob, Stump wriggled with delight. Jacob called him, and delight turned to bewilderment and then grief, as he searched the men's faces for the cause of their displeasure. His muzzle was almost scraping the dust when Jacob led him away.

"How do you tell him to go for sheep, and then make him stop?" Sewall asked.

"I just whistle." Jacob tried to demonstrate several ways of whistling but became confused. "I don't know, I just whistle."

Determined to get his firebird chicks, Sewall took a shovel and together we went back and dug out the large gray powder puffs. It was a dirty job; when we went to our Saturday night bath in the wash house we were covered with fine black soil.

The next day the weather seemed worse than ever; but about noon Sewall came back from the Parlour elated.

"The surf must be tremendous—let's go out right after dinner."

We left the house in glowing sunshine, but clouds of mist enveloped us as we walked up the flat. Making our way down the gully we set up the cameras in a previously selected crevice behind a large boulder, right in front of the rockhoppers' landing area. High tide, gigantic waves, dazzling light: it was the day we had been waiting for.

The breakers sent up towers of spray shot with rainbows. Between the crests the troughs were brilliant turquoise. The rock-hoppers hurled their solid little bodies, sleek and glistening, right toward us onto the landing rock, and hopped swiftly ashore. Often a giant wave collapsed and washed over the rock, sweeping hundreds of birds out to sea again. Struggling, they porpoised into view once more, got another foothold, and climbed to safety above the surf.

Protected by the overhang of the cliffs, we worked without pause, removing and drying the lenses every few minutes. We counted the waves and photographed every seventh one, certain that it would be the highest and carry with it the largest number of homecoming penguins. Often the waves came too close; if the tide rose we would have to scale the cliffs behind us to escape them.

Suddenly the sky blackened; squall after squall struck viciously from the open sea. The foam of the breaking waves stood out like white fangs against the threatening clouds; hundreds of little penguins were etched darkly in curtains of spray; the blue-green between the waves became momentarily more vivid, then turned an angry gray. We gave up and went home only after the squalls had merged into a steady, driving gale.

When rockhopper penguins are old enough to leave the nest, they gather in creches

During the next week the young rockhoppers grew to enormous size but still retained their down. The parents left them alone now for more extended periods each day. Gradually, one by one the chicks deserted the nests to huddle in little groups—"crèches," as they are called by ornithologists. A few adults always stood slumped in a ring around each crèche. These have sometimes been called "nursemaids," but I think that their presence at the crèches was purely incidental, for when we approached, the nursemaids showed no signs of defending the young. They were, in fact, the first to move away. Occasionally we saw a nursemaid trying to brood several big chicks in a crèche. It might have been a penguin whose chick had been killed or lost and whose urge to brood had remained unfulfilled.

When an adult, bulging with food, arrived from the sea, it went directly to its nest and trumpeted loudly. Several chicks immediately broke away from the crèche and waddled to the homecomer, which pecked at all of them but fed only one. The others returned to the crèche. Whenever we checked on our numbered rockhoppers we found that the adult always fed its own chick at the original nest site. Whether or not this was an invariable rule we had no way of knowing.

Now that there were crèches the whole colony appeared to be breaking up. During the day most of the nests were abandoned; nearly all the adults were at sea. At dusk, however, each baby was back on its own nest, where it was almost always protected by one or both parents.

In the settlement, shearing went on busily, and the atmosphere in the house was like a continuous party. On good days Jack moved Grandpa's chair to the front garden, and in especially fine weather we all stretched out around him enjoying the sun. Evenings we walked to the cliffs to check on the penguins and watch the sunset over the open sea. From the summit of Old Vic we had seen a fiery red sunset; but usually the whole island was bathed in soft pastels, in keeping with the muted hues of the Falklands. The lack of vivid color was due to the absence of dust in the atmosphere, Jack thought; there was no land nearer than ice-covered Antarctica eight hundred miles to the south, and Patagonia three hundred miles to the west. This also might have explained the absence of the aurora australis, for which we looked in vain.

The shepherds gathered the last of the ewes and lambs and herded them into a paddock by the Parlour; then they separated the lambs by driving the animals through a narrow passage to a fork where one way led to the rough sheep pasture and the other to the flat. Bob Keddle manipulated a single gate, sorting out the sheep, while Stump kept them moving down the passage.

The large fat lambs, never before without their mothers, baa-ed piteously at first, calling for the ewes which moved in the direction of the shearing shed. But not for long. Even before the frightened sheep disappeared around the hill, the lambs were gamboling on the flat. Jack admonished us to keep a sharp eye on the ditches for stray lambs, now that they were separated from the flock.

One stormy afternoon we watched the baling of the wool. Tony tossed the rolled fleeces from the loft into a burlap-lined press where Bob pushed them down and stamped on them. When the press was full, an enormous weight was lowered and pressure was applied by a handscrew, squeezing the wool down until the weight would go no lower. Then Tony bound it with steel bands, the wooden sides of the press were removed, and the burlap-covered bale was rolled to the scales where Jack stenciled it with his mark—JD,NI,23 for John Davis, New Island, 23rd bale of the season—recorded the weight (about eight hundred pounds) and noted the quality of the wool. Now it would be shipped to London, arriving in time for the May auction.

After the shearing and baling were finished, everyone on the farm would have a short holiday. Tony Felton was planning to take his family to Port Stephens in the *Overseas,* Jack's small schooner, returning in March for the dipping, when all the sheep would be gathered again and brought in to be dipped in a tobacco solution to prevent scab. In April, the rams—about sixteen in all—would be released to the flocks. During the winter that followed, the shepherds would mend fences, repair buildings, and fix horse gear, and keep on shepherding—riding the camp to check on the condition of the sheep and the feed.

Lambing would begin in September and the shepherding would become increasingly important. New Island, like the other Falkland farms, had no special facilities for looking after stray lambs; many of them were brought into the settlement and raised on bottles, and by the end of lambing each member of the family had his own pet lambs. This season's pets had been returned to the flock before we arrived.

After lambing, the ewes and lambs would be brought in for lamb-marking—notching the ear to indicate age, clipping tails, and castrating all the males except those to be used for breeding. Then shearing would begin again in November with the males and continue until the ewes with lambs were finished—about the end of January.

It was nearly mid-January now; and there were still many things to be done and many places to be seen. On Saturday afternoon Jack proposed a trip in the *Overseas* to Ship Harbour. "Sewall wants to see the kelp gulls and Jacob wants to spend the weekend at the Virgin Hotel." He set out to find Tony Felton, who doubled as a sailor, and to invite Winnie Felton and Sonja to join us.

We collected slacks for the girls and extra clothing for everyone. Jack was excited; although he was a sheep farmer and a good one, he had spent the greater part of his sixty years as a sailor in Falkland waters and his heart was with his boats. Agnes didn't entirely approve of it; she worried and watched the harbor constantly when Jack was out with his pram, even though she knew he was the best sailor in the islands.

In the trim twenty-four-foot schooner with its smooth engine we were soon around the point and entering the harbor, landing on the northern edge of a barren islet. From one side of it a cloud of gulls rose to protest our arrival. Then the *Overseas* sped off to put Jacob ashore at a beach a short distance from the Virgin Hotel.

We scattered over the islet like drops of mercury, Sewall and I in one direction toward the gulls, Agnes and Winnie to the far side to look for wild strawberries. The three children in the care of Hazel searched for skuas' nests and young to destroy.

Skuas were everywhere. Even the bold, raucous gulls were hastening back to their nests—during the brief distraction of our arrival, skuas had already stolen and eaten a number of eggs and young. Expert thieves, they were intimidated neither by the gulls nor by us. The gulls were not as stupid as penguins or shags, but they were no match for skuas. We photographed the gull chicks still in their soft, downy stage, and the adults which returned to feed and brood them, while the skuas spiraled over their own nests trying to protect them from the children.

Suddenly the lovely day turned cold, horribly cold, and the wind bore down on us in sweeping gusts. From all points of the islet we converged on the *Overseas*. The cold was so cutting that the children cried. Tony had the motor running and we were off for home. While the little boat dived and tossed, Sewall took Raymond up to the deck with Tony to watch the waves and the rest of us huddled miserably on benches in the hold.

Bob was on the jetty to meet us, and Grandpa, noting the change in the weather, had heaped peat on the fire and put the kettle on.

Gentoos in Penguin Valley

The next fair day we rode to Penguin Valley and the Virgin Hotel, carrying our equipment with us on the backs of the horses. Sewall mounted Old Sword with some hesitation; then he rode off ahead of me as easily as though he had been riding every day for twenty years. It was good to see him using his arm as naturally as though it had never been broken; the healing had been so gradual that I had hardly been aware of it.

We rode up the ridge, and circled to the far side of Ship Harbour, crossing the gentoo penguin trail on the spur of Rookery Hill; then we passed over a second ridge and followed the sheer cliffs of the western edge of the island. At one of its narrowest points, we had to dismount and lead the horses over a steep, slippery incline of clay badlands. Then the island widened again; its length, Jack said, was about seven miles from north to south; at some points its width could be measured in rods, in others it was a couple of miles. Little of it was level ground. We rode around another mountain and into a luxuriant valley, at the western edge of which stood the Virgin Hotel.

I do not know exactly what I expected it to be; what I saw was a tiny tin shanty not more than half the size of the hut on Kidney Island. It was a shelter for the shepherds when they came out to mend fences or plant tussock, and Jacob used it as a weekend retreat. Sometimes he brought the children up to spend a night. It contained everything one needed for a weekend— two bunks, a ship's stove, teakettle, blankets, dishes, and tins of food. While we unsaddled the horses, Jack boiled the kettle over a diddle-dee fire, and as there was not room for all of us in the hut, we sat in the sun outside the door and ate lunch looking out over a white beach and green flat where sheep and upland geese grazed side by side.

Jack had only half prepared us for Penguin Valley. After lunch we climbed to the rim of a steep, knifelike ridge, and looked down over the great half-moon of the valley, where colonies of gentoos made huge circular splotches against the gray-green slopes. From each colony to the broad white sand beach below stretched a bright green path alive with moving birds. Jackass penguins stood beside their burrows on the black peaty soil of the broken upper slopes, and on a lower level upland geese and their fat goslings fed around a brook where the grass grew almost rank. Overhead the skuas circled, watching and waiting.

Where the ridge curved down to the sea there were curious black mounds, standing like little ramparts torn by wind and tide. Agnes and I ran to look at them. Under the crumbling soil were masses of old bones packed in the peat.

"These are bird bones," Jack said when he caught up with us. "In the next valley there are heaps of bigger bones—of

animals I never saw." We speculated on their origin. I thought
they might have been left by whalers after they had boiled them
down, but Jack said these bones had never been boiled or pressed.
Among them Sewall found the bones of penguins and sheathbills,
well-preserved in the peat.

We walked along the beach and teased the jackass penguins
that stood rooted in their funny, serious way, refusing to yield
an inch of ground to us. They were going by their accustomed
route to the water, and anything in their way would have to move;
they would wait, but they would not step aside or turn back.

While Jack rode north to inspect fences and Agnes went to
catch goslings near the Virgin Hotel, Sewall and I got to work.
It was pleasant to be with the gentle gentoos again, after the
strident rockhoppers. They waddled up the paths and fed their
fluffy chicks, while the jackasses ambled by with an almost pain-
ful gait and disappeared into their burrows; and the skuas,
bolder and more numerous than any we had seen, snatched the
small unguarded young, tearing one apart not five feet from us.

A skua and its victim, a baby gentoo penguin

Sewall wanted a shot of a jackass penguin emerging from its burrow. As he focused on it I heard him laugh, and turned to see two baby rabbits, whose long ears had surprisingly appeared in his viewfinder. A jackass penguin came out of a neighboring burrow and stood watching them. Rabbits have been introduced on some of the Falkland Islands and have multiplied rapidly. Their favorite homes are abandoned penguin burrows, and at this time of year at least, they seem to live amicably side by side with the birds.

The ride home that night was unforgettable. We had never been away from the flat at this hour, and had not even imagined such activity as was going on around and above Ship Harbour. All the jackass penguins were home, standing in front of their burrows trumpeting. Big rabbits and little rabbits hopped all around them. From the beach came the shrill cries of the black and white oyster-catchers and the snorting-sneezing sounds of the logger ducks. The rays of the declining sun, lost to us behind Rookery Hill but still bright on the sea and the tufty islands, filled the valley with a mauve and purple light.

Hungry, late, and cold as we were, we stopped to rest the horses on the ridge above the settlement. The tiny buildings, Old Vic, and the south end of the island were all aglow. Jack, riding ahead of us, stood silhouetted against the vivid sky. How did it feel, I wondered as I watched the angular figure on the small horse, to look over one's sea-girt kingdom and find it so beautiful and so complete, to make plans for its future, to leave it a better place for one's son?

Landsend was a great sheer bluff connected to New Island by a narrow ridge. Along the northern side of the ridge, green gullies alternating with broken badlands sloped to the edge of cliffs that dropped to the sea. Jack had planted tussock to no avail. Nothing would grow there.

We stood at the edge of the cliffs and looked onto the ledges below. They were crowed with seals—large sea lions, and another kind that were smaller and darker with gentle, doglike faces. They were fur seals, Jack said. He estimated there were about eight thousand, and the number was steadily increasing. The fur seals were rigidly protected by the government, but some poaching went on in spite of this. A year before a large shipment of fur seal pelts had turned up on the New York market. They were traced to Chile, but there the trail was lost—or overlooked. In any case, the pelts had not come from Landsend. The seals there were protected by the inaccessibility of the rocks, the wild seas, and the surf that was high even on this fairly quiet day.

A cone-shaped pinnacle of rock rose from a section of the badlands. On the seaward side lived a colony of dolphin gulls. It was a spectacular location, and the birds were stunning creatures. They poked at their nests, settled comfortably on their eggs, or brooded small chicks. Adult birds returned to the colony with mouthfuls of tidbits for the young — probably shag or baby penguin. The adults squabbled and flew at each other with wings upraised, and quarreled over chicks that had wandered too far from the nests. But compared to rockhoppers they were quiet.

We ate lunch sitting on the ridge facing north; it was like eating in a three-ring circus. On the left was Landsend; on the right where the neck of land joined the island, the cliffs formed a right angle corner. A steady stream of rockhoppers moved up the almost vertical rocks to the colony that spread like a fan over the amphitheater above. At one point they scaled a perpendicular slab of rock for over thirty feet. From where we sat it looked as though they were creeping, but the telephoto lens showed that they were hopping very slowly. Now and then a climbing bird slipped and fell back, but usually caught itself in some unaccountable way—it was hard to see how it could stop once it began to slide. Two birds began to quarrel and both lost their footing and dropped to the rocks below.

An upland goose wandered past and posed nicely for its portrait; it was followed in a moment by its mate, which we almost missed because it was so well protected by its handsome brown coloration.

The ledges on both sides of the rockhopper colony were something like Coney Island. Sea lions of all sizes slept, fought, and played. Some slid quietly into the water; other raised themselves sleek and shining from the sea. Clapmatches soundly trounced their pups and bulls trounced their clapmatches. They were so closely packed together that one animal could hardly flip its tail without striking another. In among the sea lions, sheathbills walked about with precise steps searching for food, and overhead dolphin gulls fluttered.

About midafternoon great numbers of king shags assembled in the water below us for a bit of communal fishing. They strung across the water in long lines, just as they did when flying. Then they dived all at once, as if at a given signal. One moment there were shags on the water; the next there were none. When they surfaced they massed together to form a raft and floated about as one body. Over and over they formed the line, dived, and rafted. They fished between us and the afternoon sun, the water about them was flecked with gold, and their wet plumage glistened. Then they flew up from the raft in groups of twos, threes, and fours and headed in the direction of the colony with necks outstretched and wings flapping.

The rest of our stay on New Island was on borrowed time. The plane was supposed to pick us up Saturday morning. The weather was fair and we were packed and ready before breakfast. When the wireless came on and announced there would be no plane that day, we all laughed and shouted at once. It was too good to be true. "No sorrow here, Sid," Agnes told the operator at Stanley. Snapping off the set, she said, "There won't be a plane now until Monday. Today you can ride to the south end."

That afternoon Jack, Sewall, and I rode south, stopping first at an old ruin that had been the whaling station. It was built in 1908 and was active until 1916 when the whaling company moved to South Georgia. Apparently it had been cheaper to buy new machinery than to move the old: it lay there rusting and corroding; thick beams and long planks of wood, chains and windlasses, vats for boiling down oil, even pipes that led to small reservoirs; and tons and tons of coal, settled in mounds and overgrown with vegetation.

"Somebody is going to come along and find this someday and think he has discovered new coal deposits," Jack said. He occasionally came down with the *Overseas* in winter and took back a load. There was enough to last for years.

On one of the reservoirs we found a pair of yellow-billed teal with a downy young; they were drab birds, but new to us, so we photographed them. At South Pond skuas heckled us so that we almost missed a pair of Chiloë widgeons with two small young. As with the teal, both sexes were nearly alike and dull in color.

Beyond the dunes lay a beach. Great waves rolled in and

crashed over the pure white sand, and ebbed into the icy brilliance of the turquoise sea. Groups of jackass penguins, youngsters that had not quite lost their down, formed patterns on the sand, huddling close together as we passed but widening their ranks after we were some distance away. A few of them made daring sorties into the surf; some were tipped over and washed ashore, while others swam about for short distances before coming in to rejoin the group. Their plumage was exactly like the adults' except that it was steel blue where the adults' was black, and a few downy feathers gave them an unbrushed look. Strangely, although jackass penguins nested alone, they became colonial on the beach—even the adults stood together in loose aggregations, preserving some individual distance between them.

The next morning was almost too bright to believe. We went to the cliffs to expose our last rolls of film. We had brought twenty thousand feet, which seemed more than enough at the time.

Young mollymawk

The cliffs were quieter now. There were few adult penguins there, and the chicks, almost as large as their parents but still downy, had abandoned the nests for the crèches. On nearly every mollymawk nest sat a large, light-gray juvenile bird, all alone. The young king shags were so big they pushed each other off the nests. While Sewall worked I sat in a niche in the rocks looking out over the colony. A few months earlier he had said, "You'll have had enough surf and sea before you leave the Falklands," but it had not worked out that way. Neither of us had had enough.

All at once I became aware of something strange about a penguin coming toward us. It looked like a rockhopper but it stood out from the rest. What was it Edwin Cawkell had said on our first night in Stanley? "It's rare here, but you might see one. Anyway you can't mistake it. The plumes are not orange or yellow, but gold, pure gold."

"Sewall," I whispered. "Here comes a macaroni penguin!"

With the last of the film we took its picture. It was quite dirty and very dejected, but it was the only macaroni penguin we saw in the Falkland Islands.

"No plane can leave Stanley today," Sid reported over the wireless Monday morning. "The *Philomel* will call at New Island at eleven o'clock."

Sewall frowned. Agnes was excited. Sending Hazel for her horse, she said, "I'm going to the north end to shoot some rabbits for Grandma. You know how she always enjoys rabbit stew." Within an hour she was off on Pela, a gun across her saddle. Sewall went to the colony, and Hazel's school opened on schedule.

Grandpa settled himself on the front stoop, glass in hand, to watch for the *Philomel*. Today he passed up clipping skins in favor of his second job, "watching." Grandpa was always watching. He watched the milk scalding on the stove and gave warning when it was about to boil over; he watched the children playing and called for help if they strayed too far. He watched the fire and pounded with his cane when it needed peat. Grandpa was the settlement's information center. He knew where everyone was, when he left, and what time he could be expected back. The Davises wisely kept him so busy that he had no time to feel old.

He sighted the *Philomel* near the Colliers about eleven, and an hour later she entered the harbor and dropped anchor. Visiting ships were rare enough at New Island; one might have expected a little excitement, but there was none. We ate dinner as though she wasn't there. In due time Bob rowed out to get the mail and returned with three men, the captain, the cook, and a passenger. They came into the house without knocking. Jack didn't move from his place at the table.

"Have some dinner?" he said.

"We've eaten," the captain replied. They sat down. There was a long silence.

"Going to Beaver Island to beach her and clean the propeller in the sand," the captain said at last. "How's the tide?"

"No tide," Jack said. "You'll be there at least a week, until the new moon, before you have a decent tide."

There was seldom much tide in the Falklands and none that could be depended on.

There was another long silence. Jack finished his dinner and rolled a cigarette. "You could use some mutton?"

The captain nodded and the four men set out in the direction of the killing shed. Apparently the *Philomel's* visits were always taken this calmly. Agnes returned with six rabbits, and after tea the men left with mutton, rabbits, baskets of vegetables, and stacks of cakes. The captain promised to stop and pick us up on his way back if the plane had not come by then.

"The plane will come tomorrow," Sewall said positively.

When Sid told us by wireless on Tuesday that the plane couldn't fly, we were not upset, although we knew that the *Fitzroy* would sail without the New Island film. Perhaps, like the Falklanders, we had learned to accept the inevitable with grace. Edwin Cawkell talked to us at two o'clock to say good-bye and we tried to thank him again, and Mary too, for all they had done.

The plane couldn't come Wednesday because the Governor planned to lunch at Fox Bay. He never made it. The plane couldn't come Thursday because the police were summoned to San Carlos to deal with a shooting. They started and had to turn back. The plane couldn't come Friday because it had to be overhauled after twenty-four hours' flying. What flying, we wondered.

We passed the time listening to complaints pour in by wireless to John Huckle from all over the camp. One man was in Darwin and *had* to get home. The Bishop was in Fox Bay and *must* get to Stanley. The culprit in the shooting at San Carlos was a prisoner in the manager's guest room because there was no other place to put him. Wouldn't John *please* come and take him to jail? Sewall added his bit by reminding John that the penguins were growing up fast and he was out of film.

After the *Philomel* left Sewall unpacked the still moist bird skins and consulted with Jack about drying them. They decided to hang them on the clothes rack over the stove in the kitchen, on long bars that ran across the room. That night they carefully closed the kitchen door against the cats.

Some time later Raymond went into the kitchen and came out calling, "Mother, the kitchen just stinks!"

Jack was in bed; Sewall was in the Parlour. Agnes and I moved the large skins, which smelled the worst, to an outside pantry for the night. Agnes optimistically left the smaller ones. When we sat down to breakfast the next morning we were almost choked by the stench of rotting organic matter. Jack served the penguin eggs, and we began to eat.

"Look what I found!" Raymond yelled suddenly. He jumped from his chair holding a fat white grub.

"It's a blowfly maggot," Jack said, looking accusingly at Grandpa. "It must have come off your camp skins."

"There's another," Agnes said, "and . . . oh, Jack, look at your plate."

Maggots, warmed by the heat from the stove, were dropping fast now all over the table and floor. After we had got over the first paralysis we snatched the bird skins from the rack and tossed them into the garden. Suddenly the chickens raced from all corners of the yard to pick up maggots as they dropped like rain from the skins that Jack and Sewall were shaking. Stubbornly Jack brought back all the skins he thought were clean.

"If one of those things touches me," Agnes said, "I'll . . ." For once words failed her.

We forgot the morning broadcast; we forgot the plane; we plunged into what Agnes later called the "battle of the maggots." For the next few days we picked them from the bases of tails, wings, legs, and skulls—anywhere a scrap of flesh remained on Sewall's specimens—removed them with long forceps until, when we went to bed at night, we expected to find them crawling on the pillows. At first we worked carefully, but the maggots hatched too fast. Finally, disregarding all the rules for handling bird skins, we used more drastic methods. I hung the tougher skins—the logger ducks, skuas, and mollies—on the clothesline in the sun. Others I scrubbed with soap and water. Sewall daubed the more precious skins—firebirds and sheathbills—with his few remaining drops of carbon tetrachloride. Winnie donated a can of DDT, Agnes found an ancient box of insect powder.

On the second day Agnes and I escaped to ride to the north end to look for mushrooms. Tony was beginning to like me now, I thought, and gave me my first smooth ride. The brisk, cool winds of the camp dispelled the odor of maggots, and I felt clean when I rode back past the Parlour where Sewall was still doggedly working away on the skins.

We picked maggots late that night in the Parlour, and finally seemed to be getting ahead of them.

On Saturday John Huckle talked to us on the wireless.

"We can't fly today," he said. "I've arranged for you to contact the captain of the *Philomel* at two o'clock. He must be ready to leave for Stanley. Ask him to pick you up. Cheerio, over and out."

While we waited in the sitting room that afternoon to call the *Philomel*, Grandpa joined us. He was chuckling to himself. Finally he said, "I've thought and thought and now I've figured it out."

"Figured what out?"

"Why you pulled the stunt you did—the maggots."

"*Stunt!* Why did we?"

"You wanted to do something so we'd remember you," he said. "So you did something we wouldn't ever forget. Oh, those maggots dropping in Jack's breakfast! What a day!"

I'd never forget either. No other family would have made so much fun out of the maggots, I told him.

"Didn't I tell you when you came? New Island is the best place in the world." He leaned forward. "Now don't you go home and tell them that we have the worst weather in the world, because we don't."

Jack was fiddling with the wireless trying to get the *Philomel*. Instead he got the Beaver. "This is the Beaver calling New Island. This is the Beaver coming in at New Island." The plane was about to land in Tigre Bay.

Jack rowed out and brought the pilot ashore.

"It was such a nice afternoon I thought I'd just run out and pick you up," he said, climbing up the ladder onto the jetty. Didn't anyone ever listen to the wireless? He'd been trying to contact us for over an hour. Yes, he'd be glad to stop for tea. He'd always wanted to come ashore on New Island.

We took off from New Island just as the sun was disappearing behind Old Vic. We waved for as long as we could see the small figures on the jetty, straining our eyes for a last glimpse of that memorable bit of earth.

"Pettingills Parlour" on New Island

A gentoo and its growing young

Chapter 9

SUMMER WANES

I settled back in the plane, wanting to be quiet, to think about New Island. I had just spent the hardest, yet the most rewarding and exhilarating weeks of my life there; I needed time to fix them in my memory, and to ease the pain of breaking the strong ties I had formed.

But the human senses are very cruel. Almost before South Mountain had fallen behind us, the odor of decay began to permeate my consciousness. It got stronger and stronger, rising in waves about us in the small cabin. It seemed years before we landed roughly in a squall in Stanley Harbour.

Sewall and I had agreed not to mention the bird skins to the pilot, but I felt I had to explain. When Sewall left to phone Mr. Goodwin, I told the pilot they were only bird skins. He looked relieved.

When Mr. Goodwin drove up in the Land-Rover we loaded the cargo and rattled off toward town. Mr. Goodwin was already sniffing suspiciously; I began to be apprehensive: the Ship Hotel would never permit us to bring the skins there. I threw myself on Mr. Goodwin's mercy. It was not a human body he smelled, I told him, only the skeleton of a logger duck. It turned out that he had just the place to store the boxes, and in a few days we could put them aboard a charter vessel, the *Nigris N.,* which was leaving for Monte. Before it left he brought the boxes back, and Sewall, who retired to a remote corner of the garden to repack them, reported that there were very few maggots left and that only the skeleton smelled—much. Our film and the specimens both went, care of the *Nigris N.'s* first mate, to Montevideo, to be transshipped by air freight to the United States. The film was sent according to plan, but the bird skins never left the ship. Our next news of 'them came from the F.I.C. office in London. They were desperately trying to get them off their hands. The specimens, they explained, had been stored by mistake in a freight compartment that was sealed in Montevideo and never unloaded. I didn't believe that: I think the skins smelled so bad that the authorities would not allow them to be unloaded. In due time, odorless and demaggoted, they came to rest in trays in the Museum of Zoology at the University of Michigan. There were, the curator told us soberly, a surprising number of big dead flies in the boxes they came in.

After three days in Stanley we went back to Charles Point to spend a week among the gentoo penguins. The whole camp was a little greener, and Mount Lowe did not look quite so barren. But the wind still drove through the hut, violent storms came down from the mountain, and the fireplace smoked. This time we had Edwin's Tilley stove with us, and if the shanty had been wind-proof the fumes might have overcome us.

The gentoo penguins had changed too. On the beach at Rabbit Cove there were hundreds of them lounging where in October there had rarely been more than thirty at one time. The colony, when we first saw it, was deserted except for the young, grown big now and beginning to get their adult feathers. They looked shaggy, moth-eaten, and rather silly with tufts of down clinging to them, and sleek new undercoat showing through in patches. They were nearly grown up but still awkward and not quite sure of themselves; they struck us as typical teenagers.

They had an insatiable curiosity. A group approached us and stood motionless, then circled us, and silently stared. A few bolder ones came near enough to peck at our boots. At last I had my circle of admiring penguins. But not for long—suddenly the whole whole gang, overcome with boredom, left in a rush to look over some old bones. Some stumbled and fell, waving their flippers wildly.

The teenagers spent a great deal of time sleeping. A few of them napped on their feet, bills tucked under flippers, slumped bodies swaying in the wind; but most of them lay stretched full length on their bellies, totally relaxed, undisturbed by the wind ruffling their down. None of them slept very long; one would walk about waking up others, tripping over an extended foot or flipper, or even taking a mischievous nip.

Sewall among the young gentoos

Although the young penguins moved in gangs or slept in loose groups, the crèche system, as we had seen it among the rockhoppers, was no longer in effect here. There were still a few adults in the colony—one for about every twenty-five young—but they only loafed or slept. Although the season was far advanced, three adults still sat on eggs and several still guarded very small young.

About four in the afternoon, adult penguins, so stuffed with shrimps they could hardly waddle, began to arrive from the beach, first in twos and threes, later in increasing numbers. The hungry youngsters came to life, running around in circles and jumping up and down. Many of them crowded to the side of the colony where the adults arrived, and some even went down the path to meet the homecoming birds.

The first youngsters to beg food from an adult were generally rebuffed testily with quick jabs from the bill. Each adult apparently had to find the right youngster in the right place, and this took time. As a rule an adult would approach a youngster, eye it closely, and then start to run away. The youngster invariably followed it, and the birds would run all around the colony. Finally the adult stopped, opened its beak, and poured shrimp into the youngster's gaping mouth.

A gentoo, returned from the sea, feeds its young

If a youngster failed to follow the adult as it ran away, the latter would go back and feed it a morsel, just to start the chase. Sometimes four or five young birds chased a single adult that ran until all but one had given up; this one was promptly fed. The young birds chasing the adult, which tried to run fast on its stubby feet, was the funniest of all the penguin performances.

We could not make out whether adult birds always fed their own offspring. They certainly seemed to try. Some of them, on entering the colony, would go directly to old nest sites, as if expecting to find the youngsters at home. By six o'clock, when the birds were trooping in by the dozens, there was such confusion that feeding the right youngsters seemed impossible. The ravenous young birds would chase any adult that came along, and adults were feeding birds everywhere.

Dolphin gulls, which had been rare in the colony back in October, now walked boldly among the feeding penguins, darting quickly between adult and youngster, so that the shrimps spilled on the ground and the gulls could snatch them before the penguins knew what was going on. The young ones could never recover the food once it was dropped. Like the Cawkells' bird Pengy, they never even tried to retrieve food from the ground.

The sky cleared now and then during that week, but not for very long at a time, and when we could not photograph penguins, we took shots of storms and scenery. I collected mosses, samples of balsam bog, and some of the flowering plants. The bright yellow sand cabbage still bloomed between the pasture and the beach, and a kind of wild onion raised its fluffy head above the soil near the hut. In the tidal pools below the rocks off the point we found lumps of purple coral; we skimmed a few aquatic beetles from peat bog pools but found no waterbugs.

Summer was waning. Black and white oystercatchers searched for crustaceans along the edge of the water, but no longer did their stiff-legged dance; Falkland plovers moved with their full-grown families to the uplands above the beaches; the logger ducks no longer scolded us as they fished off shore with their broods of large young ones.

The shingle of Rabbit Cove was occupied almost entirely by gentoos, but the beach west of the hut near which there was a small colony of gentoos was thronged with both gentoo and jackass penguins, large, closely packed circles of young jackasses, and looser groups of adults. The gentoos moved en masse to the beach each day and returned home in the evening. Some of the young of both species that had shed their down were timidly exploring the water.

One clear afternoon after a heavy, drenching rain—the first downpour we had had—we went to the gentoo colony determined to get pictures of the young chasing adults. Overhead the light was lovely but the scene on the ground, of puddles and mud and dirty young penguins, was distressing. "We can't take pictures today," I said. "They look horrible. Look at that messy . . ."

The messy young penguin at that moment tripped over its own feet and fell into a puddle.

"This will be better than the chasing," Sewall said, laughing. "Let's get to work."

The young penguins, we realized, had never seen water like this before, and they were delighted. A group stood on the edge of a puddle and dabbled their toes in it. Then, as if someone had said "I dare you" they all raced through it splashing. Penguins dashed about all around us; one would fall down or be pushed, and knock over others. Then they bounced up and waded some more. Some even dared to lie in the puddles on their bellies with their flippers fanning the air. Mud streaked their white fronts and matted their fuzzy down. They were too excited to take naps, and they ignored the adults returning with food.

We got no chasing pictures that day; we took them later; and we also got quantities of pictures of birds porpoising landward in the late afternoon when the low rays of the setting sun intensified the color of the sea and beach. I hated leaving Charles Point just when the young penguins had reached such an exciting stage of growth; but we had to meet the *Gambler* in Stanley for another trip to Kidney Island.

At the Ship Hotel we found a cablegram. The first of the film had arrived in Hollywood, but where, Erwin Verity wanted to know, were the scenarios? I was glad I had made carbon copies. The next day we had another cable: the second lot of film had arrived, and all had been viewed. Everyone was delighted; but where were the letters explaining the films?

I thought of all the beautiful stamps I had pasted on those letters. Edwin Cawkell had been right; they had been stolen. But the films, at any rate, were safe.

Sewall conferred with the captain of the *Gambler*. We were to go to Kidney Island for a week, return to Stanley for one day, and then embark on a five-day cruise down the east coast, with a stop at Bleaker Island, where Arthur F. Cobb had gathered most of the material for his book, *Birds of the Falkland Islands*.

When I went to the store to buy supplies for Kidney Island, I ran into the Bishop, whom we had met at Mr. Rowe's. We had already got acquainted by wireless: he had been stranded at Fox Bay while we were at New Island waiting for the plane, and he had listened to us on the wireless. We had beaten him to Stanley by twenty-four hours. With headquarters at Buenos Aires and all of

South America south of the Amazon as his diocese, he was used to rugged traveling; he had gone the length of Chile to board the *Fitzroy* at Puntas Arenas because trouble between Argentina and Uruguay prevented his going to Montevideo.

The Bishop took charge of ordering our food for Kidney Island, recommending extra tins of kidney soup and large boxes of chocolate bars. He insisted on the clerk's opening a case of tinned spaghetti that had just arrived from the jetty, and made him give me a whole dozen of the precious oranges. Of course, he said, we needn't worry about food on Kidney Island; we could always eat tussock—the hearts, boiled whole, tasted like asparagus.

When I ran into Freddy White, he told me the place was crawling with North Americans—he had just brought another one down from Monte. Later, back at the hotel, when I heard a voice ask in a familiar accent, "Please, miss, have you a room available?" I turned and asked, "How's everything at home?"

I could see the young man's disappointment at having traveled to the ends of the earth only to meet another American. But he was undaunted. There was no room at the Ship but for the time being he was comfortable on the *Fitzroy*. He was from New York. He liked Stanley and was going to stay two years if he had to dig a hole in a peat bog and live there.

I felt like saying, "Brother, this is a nice day. Wait till you see . . ." but I didn't want to disillusion him. He went off whistling.

On February 12 the *Gambler* took us to Kidney Island. We found the hut, unoccupied since our visit in December, neat and tidy. Aside from a sea lion that had to be evicted from the front garden, everything was in order.

The tussock, grown rank since December, had almost obliterated our path, and recent rains had turned the colony in the grass into a stinking swamp. Feathers floated about in the putrid atmosphere. It was a relief to reach the fresh, cool air of the open cliffs.

Sewall looked about. "Good lord! They're molting!"

All the birds in sight wore patches of loose old feathers that made them appear much larger; new feathers underneath were pushing out the old. Their heads and backs had turned an ugly brown, their white fronts were filthy, their red eyes dull. Dazed and stupid, they just sat looking rather sick and uncomfortable.

During molting, rockhoppers are hungry and irritable

Those with life enough in them to hop away from us cast feathers that were wafted out to sea or were caught in updrafts and, swirled by the gusts that eddied about the cliffs, accumulated in windrows among the rocks. We churned up feathers with every step. It was as if a thousand pillows had been ripped open and dumped over the colony.

One rockhopper moved aside to avoid being stepped on and bumped into its neighbor. This started the usual chain reaction; rockhopper pushed rockhopper, fights ensued, and feathers yanked out by beakfuls flew about us in a snowstorm.

We went to work at once taking pictures of adults and young in all stages of molting. No two birds shed in exactly the same way, and no two of them looked alike. Most often the feathers from face and flippers were shed first, thus many rockhoppers had glossy little heads atop big fluffy bodies. Others sported strange headdresses created by a few tufts of old feathers that remained here and there. There were, I discovered to my surprise, no

A molting rockhopper

black feathers; only the tips of feathers were black, overlapping one another so closely that they made a solid black area.

Sewall estimated that the molting process took at least three weeks. During this period the penguins' plumage was not waterproof; they had to stay on land and consequently go without food. Hunger made them cross and more quarrelsome than ever. The cackling in the colony now was largely an uncontrolled expression of bad temper. The molting birds were especially resentful of a minority group—the ones that had completed their shedding and, all sleek and trim in their new winter outfits, hopped along the cliffs and down to the sea. The birds that were still molting never missed a chance to take a poke at them as they passed.

The young rockhoppers were so inconspicuous that we hardly noticed them. Most of the chicks had lost their second down and were in their first full plumage—like the adults' but a dark blue-gray instead of black. There were no crèches, no gang play such as we had seen among the gentoos. The young just sat still. It was safer that way. They were sure to be pecked by their ifritable elders if they moved about.

Each day as more and more birds finished molting, their new plumage glistened, their brilliant red eyes sparkled, and their tufts were bright yellow again. Soon, when the shedding was over, all the rockhoppers would desert the cliffs to spend the winter in their true home, the sea. Land was only a temporary residence to which they were forced to come and build their nests and rear their young.

The weather that week was the best all summer. Twice we ate lunch in the yard. One day the thermometer nearly reached 70° and I sun-tanned for an hour on the beach not far from the old sea lion. He roared once when he saw me coming, then turned over and continued his nap.

The pressure was off the wild life. Only a few jackass penguins ambled by. The logger ducks raised only a token protest when I came near their two big ducklings, all that were left of a brood of eight. Wrens, tussockbirds, and robins leisurely flipped over bits of kelp; their nests were empty, they had no extra mouths to feed. Only the kelp goose was still excitable; she took off in a rage after a lone female that must have ventured too near her gander, and chased the intruder clear across the harbor. Kidney Island was heavenly that afternoon.

One calm evening we walked at sunset to the western end of the island to look for sooty shearwaters and shoemakers—large petrels which, Edwin said, came in at dusk during the nesting season. From the top of some barren, jagged rocks we had a good view of the tussock-covered slope and the open ocean. Not a bird was to be seen in the air, but at sea far off shore, we saw a long, dark streak that ran parallel to the northern side of the island. Moments later the streak rose into the air and we realized it was a host of countless birds. They came nearer, rising, wheeling, then settling again on the water. It was an odd time for shags to be fishing, I thought. The sun had set, and the afterglow was fading fast. The birds rose, wheeled, and settled again; then in their flight they passed high over the island, and circled lower and lower until they were right above us. We ducked as the big birds swooshed swiftly by, just missing us. Then a crashing sound made me jump. With no decrease in

Sewall on a rocky ledge at Kidney Island

speed a bird had plunged straight into the tussock. There was another crash and another; birds were diving into the tussock all around us. The air teemed with birds, the diving accelerated. Then suddenly it was all over; there was not a bird in sight except an oystercatcher running in the shadow along the beach and the faint outline of a heron fishing from the kelp. The crashing birds were deep in their burrows under the tussock.

I trembled, recalling another night on Kidney Island when I had stood signaling and some big birds had rushed by my light.

When Sewall caught his breath, he told me they were shoe-makers and sooty shearwaters, probably the same birds that had frightened me so that October night. I had not heard any crashing then, probably because I had been standing on the very edge of the flight circle.

"If it had been like this," I told him, "we'd have stayed on Kidney Island a lot longer. I would have been too scared to move again."

We came back every night the rest of the week, and Sewall collected two adult specimens. One day he went into the tussock to dig out some young. The burrows were hard to open; the narrow tunnels twisted beneath the tussock bogs for more than an arm's length. We dug under one bog and around it, trying to undermine it and tip it over. The bog was firmly rooted and wouldn't budge.

"Just run your hand down that burrow and see if it comes out the other side," Sewall said across the bog.

I thrust my bare hand in, felt something with feathers on it, and withdrew quickly. Sewall came around, put his heavily gloved hand in the burrow, and pulled out a surprised jackass penguin, its sharply hooked beak open and ready for action.

"According to Edwin, your hand should be in ribbons."

The ruffled bird was molting. Its young had left for the beach and the jackass penguin had retired to its burrow to remain until it had its new plumage. We stuffed the bird back in its hole and went on digging until we found a young sooty shearwater.

Exploring the eastern end of the island, we came upon a small sheltered cove with a rough boulder beach protected by two broken, slab-sided cliffs that projected far out on either side. On the tide line of the beach a pair of black oystercatchers fed mussels to one full-grown young, splitting open the shells and ripping out the meat with their chisel-like bills. Between feedings they scolded us shrilly. A few black-chinned siskins, the first we had seen on Kidney Island, darted in and out of the overhanging tussock, beneath which lay three ancient sea lions. Two of these sad creatures retreated to the water at our approach. The bird was too weary to move; he merely yawned, revealing a toothless mouth.

We brought our cameras, and while Sewall photographed on the beach I climbed along the hazardous rocks of the southern point, a series of pinnacles between which the surf rolled and splashed. Toward the end of the point turkey vultures roosted on tussock bogs that clung precariously atop the steepest heights. I scrambled high enough to look over into the next cove. The small bay, almost a duplicate of the one where Sewall was working, was full of sea lions—great bulky males, smaller, slimmer clapmatches, and pups of all sizes. They lay all over the rocks and beach and up in the tussock as far as I could see. This was the source of the roaring I heard every night, the lair of the animals that swam beneath the rockhopper cliffs. Evidently the old sea lions we met on the beaches and in the tussock were only outcasts, driven from the colony by the younger males.

We could not bring the heavy cameras out here, but I wanted the Leica for some still shots. In my haste to get back, I jumped from a rock right into a family of black-crowned night herons, two adults and three young not long out of the nest. We were all startled. The birds slipped and clawed and flopped among the rocks. Cautiously I crept up on them and shooed them toward the photographer on the beach. Sewall saw us coming and adjusted the camera. Then the herons reached the edge of the beach and stepped into a tidal pool that the black oyster-catchers considered their own. Like three black devils the latter flew screeching at the poor muddled herons, which, hemmed in by the cliffs on one side and the sea on the other, turned back toward me and flapped past me to their own territory halfway to the end of the point.

"Make them do it again," Sewall commanded.

I made them do it again, not once but three times, but I never could drive them beyond the tidal pool on the beach. By the time Sewall was satisfied I had forgotten about the sea lions.

One day while cutting a moss specimen from the base of a tussock bog I uncovered a beautiful pink berry about the size of a raspberry. A Falkland Island strawberry, I thought, the same as some small, hard, half-green berries I had tasted on New Island, only ripened. It had seeds like a blackberry and its flavor was nondescript—a little sweet and earthy. When the berries were doused with sugar and sherry, the sherry was wonderful.

They grew most thickly east of the hut in an open area that

had once been cleared for experimental gardens to supplement the Stanley food supply, a project long since abandoned. There I came on a number of water holes or wells, about a foot in diameter. Filled with stinking water and overgrown with grass they were perfect booby traps. I discovered the first one by stepping into it and sinking down over my high boot. I was attracted to others by the muffled cries of young jackass penguins that had fallen in. Sewall helped me fish out one poor half-dead, waterlogged bird and remarked that from the stench several others must have drowned in the same well. But he scoffed at my fear of stepping in one and breaking a leg.

Early in the evening the short-eared owls began their nightly forays. Sewall went out to photograph them in the tussock that bordered on the area pitted with hidden wells. I had no wish to go out at night, not on Kidney Island—I was afraid of stepping on sleeping sea lions, I was afraid of weird sounds, I was afraid of the wells. But I followed him with the flashlight, trying to catch an owl in its beam. If we could spot an owl and hold the beam on it, there was time to take several flash pictures before the bird flew away. A short-eared owl, its eyes very round and yellow, staring out from behind crisscrossed blades of tussock, made a picture worth getting, I had to admit.

The trouble was that the owls teased us. We would find one, take several shots, and then decide from the silence that the owls had gone, and return to the hut. Once we were settled down to read or write notes, the owls would begin calling again all around the hut. Sewall would ignore them as long as he could, then sigh, pick up the camera, and venture into the night again. This time he really would step in a well and break his leg, I thought, and followed him in a slightly worse temper than before.

One night after he had taken pictures, Sewall collected two owls. I thought that would end the night-prowling, but the next night there were six owls where two had been, and we knew why. They were feasting on wingless crickets that were abundant around the hut. The stomachs of the owls shot the previous night had been full of them. This raised my opinion of the owls, as I had found too many dead crickets floating in the thick algae-filled water of the rain barrel. As long as the owls ate them, I did not care how much they disturbed the night calm.

Friday, one week after our arrival, was a strange day—windless, with some light rain in the afternoon. That evening the sky cleared and we sat awhile outside the hut watching the moon. It had been our best week. We had more than enough pictures of rockhoppers and plenty of small birds and scenery. Tomorrow we would take a few more shots of tussock and cliffs and gulls fishing in the harbor; we would collect a few crickets from the grass and crustaceans from the kelp, and some specimens of yellow flowers that were blooming around the tussock bogs and the wild celery that grew in a tangle on one side of the hut; we would gather tussock seeds for a friend in Stanley and wild strawberries for the table at the Ship Hotel. We would have plenty to do, and Sunday we would go back to Stanley.

A slight breeze from the northeast floated across the island, bringing with it the distinctive odor of the rockhopper colony. Dampness rose from the wet, decaying vegetation and hung in the air. The full moon, very large and bright, was circled by a great golden ring.

"That's a sign of bad weather," I remarked.

"Nonsense," Sewall said. "Superstition born of ignorance."

Saturday morning seemed to prove him right. It was lovely and we had no trouble finishing our work before lunch. That afternoon it rained and the wind blew from the north. When dinner was over I surveyed my larder prior to packing and noted with satisfaction that we had used up most of the perishable food. The bacon, eggs, and butter we would finish Sunday morning. Putting aside enough bread for toast, I tore the remainder of the loaf into small bits and put them out for a robin that came to feed at the window. Then I added all the crackers and cookies. The leftover tinned food I packed in a carton to return to the shop. There was not much—a few tins of beans, soup, fruit, and a small Danish ham. We had plenty of Scotch. Both Sewall and I had bought some, each thinking the other would forget. The extra we would save for the cruise down the coast.

On Sunday morning a storm broke with wind and rain so bad that we never even bothered to look for the *Gambler*. By night the gale was so violent that we skipped our twilight vigil with the shearwaters and forgot the owls.

Monday morning dawned cloudy but fairly calm. After a rather slim breakfast of oranges, ham, and coffee, we packed all the duffel and waited impatiently for the ship. Surely, we told each other, there was nothing to prevent her coming today. In the late afternoon, when there was still no sign of the *Gambler,* we pinned a note for the captain on the door of the hut and walked to the rockhopper colony for a last look at the shedding birds. One glance from the cliffs told us why the *Gambler* had not come. The ocean was tumultuous, without pattern or rhythm. Spindrift rose in clouds from mountainous waves.

Rockhoppers rest precariously on steep rock slopes

For the first time I began to be concerned about the food supply. We had finished the cheese and oranges for lunch. Sewall watched the robin pecking away at the heap of scraps outside the window and said, "That bird has had more to eat today than I have." We could get by one more day, I decided. It was awkward to be without bread, cereal, crackers, or cookies. Extravagantly I opened a tin of beans for dinner.

"This is Washington's Birthday," Sewall noted. "Where's the cherry pie?"

"Eat this and thank the Bishop," I retorted and tossed him half a candy bar.

That night the storm really broke. It bore down on our island, not steadily but with squalls so violent and so frequent that we began to wonder if the hut was well anchored to the soil. The thermometer was down in the 30's.

On Tuesday morning we watched the thrashing tussock from our tiny window and craned our necks for a glimpse of Mt. Lowe over which the dark clouds gathered before they swept down upon us. We stayed in the hut until we had claustrophobia; then we ventured short distances—Sewall to collect birds, I to hunt for wild strawberries.

As I knelt down to search for the small fruit, blades of tussock grass slapped me in the face. I recalled what the Bishop had said: it was wonderful raw, like asparagus when cooked. I selected a thick green stalk and peeled off the outer blades until I came to the soft white heart within, a piece about as big as my little finger. Gingerly I took a bite of it. It was good—excellent, in fact, crisp with almost an almond flavor. I decided to fix some for hors d'oeuvres with our drinks. With a sheaf of tussock and a cup of strawberries, I returned to the hut where Sewall was already skinning his bag of three small birds.

"Better save the breasts," I suggested. "They might come in handy for breakfast." I knew he was hungry; lunch had been only a tin of soup diluted with water, tinned fruit, and tea.

I sat down outside the door to peel the tussock. A mound of green blades rose around me but the pile of white hearts accumulated very slowly. It was frightfully cold; the wind was blowing around corners again. My fingers were so numb that I finally gave up.

I put the tussock on a plate and placed it before my husband. "We've finally come to it," I said. "Do have a piece of tussock."

He nibbled a stalk. "Wonderful," he exclaimed. "Remarkable woman to think of this." We had a gay cocktail hour.

When I started to add coal to the fire that Sewall had jacked up for cooking dinner, the box was almost empty. I looked at the few lumps with sinking heart. "There's hardly enough coal here to last the night. What will we do if . . .?"

"They'll come for us tomorrow," Sewall assured me confidently.

"Mr. Rowe knows we're out of supplies. If the *Gambler* isn't back, he'll send someone else."

On that note of optimism I sliced the last of the Danish ham—very thinly. Tussock hearts were appetizing, not filling. The small portion of ham, leftover beans, and some wild strawberries—with sugar or sherry—did nothing to satisfy our appetites, sharpened as they were by the cold.

After dinner we decided to do something about the fuel—"just in case," we told each other. Sewall chopped up all the odd pieces of wood lying about—a few old boxes, some boards, and the poles we had used as markers on the path to the rockhopper colony. Recalling how Mac, the sailor who had guarded our cameras after the broken-arm episode, had sneered at our coal and said he would rather burn peat, I went out into the wind and cut damp slices of turf from the base of a tussock bog. We used the coal and wood that night and heaped the peat around the stove to dry.

Tuesday night was horrible. We slept fitfully as the wind rushed against the hut and howled over the island. Although the storm had slackened somewhat by morning, we knew it was futile to expect any ship that day. After a breakfast of tiny breasts of tussockbirds and robins simmered in water—we had no fat—and the last of the coffee, we again faced the problem of fuel. The tussock peat burned very well—too well. Poof! and the stove was empty. It boiled the kettle but did little to warm the hut.

Together we set out for the windswept beach—Sewall with a gun for birds, I with a burlap bag for driftwood. We had seen precious little; there was no place for it to come from. Ships were few and the nearest land area was far away. The beach that had teemed with birds such a short time ago was lifeless. The wind was frightful. Thoroughly chilled we returned to the hut empty-handed except for a few small pieces of wood. From then on we took advantage of every break in the weather to cut tussock peat.

That night I boiled a big bunch of tussock hearts and served them with the last bit of salad cream. Sewall's only comment was "The mayonnaise is wonderful."

Thereafter we ate our tussock raw. As I peeled and peeled I recalled what Mr. Rowe had told me about two American sailors who were shipwrecked on a tussock island. They lived on nothing but tussock for fourteen months and, when they were rescued, were in excellent physical condition. I peeled with renewed vigor.

"We'll eat up their whole darned island," Sewall remarked, "if they don't come for us soon."

On Wednesday, February 24, the storm still raged and the cold became more intense. We began to wonder how long this sort of thing was apt to last. Could the *Gambler* have been wrecked in the storm? Just how dependable was her captain anyway? Would he send someone else if he couldn't come himself? Would we reach Stanley in time for the next *Fitzroy,* about March 7? Would this abominable wind ever stop?

The cruise down the east coast was definitely out now.

"If I ever set foot in Stanley, I'll not board another ship except the *Fitzroy,*" I declared. "Do you realize that if we miss this sailing, we may have to stay in the Falklands a long time? The *Fitzroy* is booked solid until a year from next July?" I stomped out for a pail of water.

Even the water supply was low and very green. The storms that raged over the island seemed to have plenty of rain, sleet, hail, and snow, but very little moisture dripped from our roof. I returned with my pail only half full. There was a barrel on the other side of the hut, so overgrown with tussock that I could not reach it. Sewall advised me not to try. He had found two dead wrens floating in it. As for the barrel we were using, I hoped we would not reach the bottom; Edwin had told me he'd dropped three cakes of soap in it.

During a lull in the storm that afternoon, we took off for the protected eastern cove. Even this sheltered beach was empty except for the three black oystercatchers which Sewall refused to kill. He had got too used to them, he said. Instead he set up the cameras and photographed the violent surf striking the outer upthrusts of rocks beyond the points and the ever changing clouds that sped across the sky. We noticed a flutter of wings and a swallow dropped almost beside us—a creature too tired and beaten to go on. Sewall picked it up and held it in his hand.

"A Chilean swallow," he said. "Blown from South America." We looked at each other. "This must be a very big storm."

Two large mullet swam in the shallows close to the shore. We cursed ourselves for not having a hook and line. Sewall dropped his camera and ran for his gun, but it was too late. They swam away and we never saw any more.

Rain and hail drenched us in the tussock, but before we reached the hut a gorgeous rainbow arched the sky, vivid and beautiful.

The cold and wet were forgotten. We photographed the rainbow and, after it faded, walked home briskly. The storm was over. We changed to dry clothes, made hot tea on the primus, and stuffed the stove with peat.

Then with renewed enthusiasm I busied myself changing the papers on the plants I was trying to dry.

"I've got a nice collection of the plants of this island," I said. "Tussock, yellow flowers, wild celery. . . ." I paused. "Wild celery . . . wonder how it would taste?"

I ran outside, pulled up a plant, and nibbled on the stem.

That night I boiled a large pan of celery and poured over it a sauce made from the dregs of the last can of evaporated milk, a lot of water, and all the flour I could shake from the small paper bag. It was not very good. It was horrid, in fact, strong and tough, but we ate it all, plus a few warmed-up beans and a quarter of a candy bar.

Later when I showed my plant collection to a botanist at the University of Michigan Biological Station, I pointed with pride to the specimen of wild celery.

"We ate lots of this when we were hungry on Kidney Island," I said.

"Good Lord, you didn't!" he exclaimed. "You both should have known better than that. Certain of this carrot family are deadly poison. Never, never again, touch anything that resembles it in the field. It might have killed you both."

The wild celery didn't kill us, but I think it caused Sewall to talk of penguins with a strange gleam in his eye. Penguins would be easy to collect, he told me. They would provide plenty of meat and the fat I had been wishing for. What about a penguin?

"If it comes to eating penguin," I pleaded, "please don't tell me. Just skin it and clean it. I'll cook it, but if I *know* I'm eating penguin, I'll feel like a cannibal—as if I were eating my little brother." He never mentioned it again.

Hunger made us jittery and, although we tried to keep busy,

the hours in the small cold hut passed very slowly. Strange to have so much of time that had once been so precious.

We wrote in our journals and read everything from Murphy's *Oceanic Birds* to the ancient newspapers between my plants. Sleep, which with all our strenuous activity had presented no problem except getting enough, became broken and dream-laden because of our forced leisure and constant hunger. This was quite different from going on a diet with a pantry full of good food. This was real, gnawing hunger. We found ourselves talking constantly about food—about steak while we were eating wild strawberries. It was all my fault. I cursed myself for my parsimony. By day we stared greedily at the sheep and cattle grazing on the mainland just across the channel. By night we watched the lighthouse and the glow in the low clouds above Stanley and thought of the mutton roasting in the ovens. We would not starve but. . . . I tightened my belt another notch. Anyway it was streamlining my figure.

On Thursday when the rainbow had not kept its promise and the storm began all over again, Sewall became desperate for something to do. He took from the meat safe outside the door all the filthy pans, dishes, and silver that we had tossed there on our first dismal arrival, and boiled and scrubbed and scoured them clean. I watched him with consternation, recalling what I had heard about people taking leave of their senses under stress.

I was relieved when the rain ceased after lunch and he agreed to stop grubbing at the pans and walk to the eastern cove to look at the seals. Actually it was a very bad idea, for the surf ran high and we were drenched with spray before we reached the point where we could see the seal cove. At first we noticed only dolphin gulls, lined up in row on row along the tops of the thin sheets of upright rocks, and then the sea lions, hundreds of them. The cove was packed—a seething mass of sea lions— many more than I had seen on my previous visit. All the seals from miles around had taken refuge from the storm in this cove.

"Wonder how a baby sea lion would taste?" I asked.

"Probably not bad, but I'm not sure we could get down there. Anyway I left the gun on the beach."

Slowly we made our way back to the shore where there was

not a bird, not even an oystercatcher, in sight. Sewall picked up his gun and we started for home.

That night there was nothing but boiled, sauceless, butterless wild celery, nothing except tussock and strawberries. I looked at the one remaining tin—beans—hesitated, and decided not to open it yet. The worst part of this isolation was not knowing how long it might last. After dinner Sewall went to the beach with his gun and returned with a scrawny night heron.

I simmered the breasts for his breakfast and watched half with greed and half with disgust as he tried to chew the tough muscles. The carcass of the heron went into a pot of boiling water and all day long I fed the fire with peat to keep it simmering. The meat never became tender enough to leave the bones. That night I added lots of celery, the last half can of kidney soup, and a few grains of salt. The stew tasted fair, but for two people who had eaten practically nothing all day long, there was not nearly enough. We ate slowly, trying to kill time, and because we had to. The strips of meat were like rubber bands.

That evening we decided to signal the lighthouse and when dinner was over, climbed the ridge. Exactly one half hour after we saw the first beams from the light (a prearranged time) we flashed regular signals with both the flashlight and Stroboflash. Very soon the rotating light paused in its turning and shone directly upon us. Our flashes had been seen.

When the answer came from the lighthouse, I began to shake and then to laugh and cry. All the fears that had never once showed during the previous Kidney Island adventure rose to the surface and I wept from relief—this time I was not alone.

The weeping was over before we reached the hut, but the shaking continued—no doubt from the cold. Sewall made me sit close to the fire while he brewed the panacea for all ills—tea. Then we talked of Maine and Minnesota and of Bermuda and Iceland until it was time for bed.

I dreamed of a carnival that night—of thick, juicy hamburgers sizzling on a griddle, of lemonade and cotton candy. Before I had a chance to taste anything, I was racing an airplane— a toy airplane suspended by wires from the top of a pole. Faster we raced and faster until. . . .

"They're here!" I heard Sewall shout above the roar of a motor. "They're here."

I sat bolt upright. In the dim light I saw a white streak dash out the door. The sound of the plane crossed from dream to reality and came closer and closer to the hut.

"Come on out," Sewall called. "Come out so that he can see you're all right." The plane passed over the hut.

I went from sleeping bag to jeans and jacket in one jump and thrust my feet into my sneakers. The next time the plane came over I was outside brandishing a pan and spoon. The pilot waved.

"He's only checking to make sure we're both well," I said. "He can't land here. Edwin said so."

"But he is landing," Sewall exclaimed as he struggled to pull on his jeans over his long underwear.

We ran to the edge of the bluff and saw the plane settle in the harbor and taxi toward shore. The pilot jumped out and held the craft by one pontoon as we ran down the path. It was John Huckle.

"Good morning," he said. "If you two keep this up, I'm going to start a taxi service. How about some breakfast?"

"Breakfast!" I nearly screamed. "No breakfast here. We're hungry!"

He laughed. "I know it. The whole town knows it. Come on, Mrs. Pettingill, I can only take one at a time."

I thought of getting lipstick and a comb and issuing instructions to Sewall, but John wouldn't let me. The calm would not last. In no time we were off, leaving Sewall alone on the beach. If the weather held, John would come back for him as soon as he had delivered me.

"Did you eat a penguin?" John asked over the roar of the motor. I shook my head. "You should have. I did once. They're not bad."

Flying in this little plane was like flying on a magic carpet with a motor. It was new, a rebuilt Auster, an auxiliary craft, used when the Beaver was grounded.

The sunrise was gorgeous, all red and gold. The peaks of Mount William and the Twin Sisters were covered with snow. As we flew over the gentoo colony on Charles Point, the birds scattered in disorder at the sound of the plane.

In just seven minutes we settled in the harbor right in front of the Ship Hotel. I got out and, standing hip-deep in the icy water, turned the tiny plane around; and John flew off to pick up Sewall. The sun, just touching the red-roofed houses, made the little town the most beautiful sight in the world. Then the wind came up, ruffling the harbor and sending black clouds streaming across the sky from the southwest.

Dirty and forlorn, hair uncombed, face untouched, jeans streaming with water, I walked up to the hotel just as a lone workman rounded the corner, carrying a lunch box.

"May I help you?" he asked faintly, his British aplomb intact in this extremity.

"No, thank you," I replied with equal poise, as if I had just come in from a customary morning dip, and staggered into the hotel.

Mollymawks and Rockhoppers

Whalebone arch

Chapter 10

LAST DAYS

After Sewall had arrived and we had gone downstairs to a real breakfast with bacon, toast, porridge, and coffee, and answered all the questions of the anxious manager and the guests, we felt a letdown. Wandering uneasily from bedroom to sitting room, we did not know what to do. There was so much to be done before we left, but at the moment there was nothing. Our cameras were still on Kidney Island, where they would remain until the *Gambler,* sitting out the bad weather in an isolated harbor on the east coast, could come back to pick them up. Our cruise was definitely off. . . .

I stuffed the stove with peat and was sitting down with an ancient copy of *The London Illustrated News* when a familiar voice came from the downstairs passage.

"Ellie, Sewall, where are you?"

It was Agnes Davis. In a moment she was up the stairs and all three of us were laughing and talking at once.

"I never intended to leave home," she told us, "but it was lonesome after you left. When the plane brought Mally and the baby back, I decided there was no sense letting the pilot come back to Stanley alone. Helen's with me. We got here just before the storm broke and can't get back."

She was staying with Grandma Davis, but she was seldom there. She had found a horse and someone to ride with her. She had been attending parties and bazaars and had done lots of shopping. . . . She had found out that we were back when she went to the wireless station to talk to Jack. "You can't sneak into this town even at sunrise." Jack was worried, she said; Tony Felton had left Port Stephens five days ago in the *Overseas*

and wasn't back yet. . . . She talked on until, breathlessly she
realized it was time for dinner at Grandma Davis's and left,
promising to meet me for tea later.

We were almost the only customers in the Stanley Cottage
that afternoon. Streaming rain made rivers on the window panes;
glowing peat sent light into the darkened room. With Grandma
Davis and Helen we sat and talked on about our experiences on
New Island. Grandma, stern and straight, listened incredulously,
her piercing bright eyes—so like Jack's—twinkling and her golden
earrings sparkling as she nodded. She had always refused even
to consider a visit to New Island; now she was almost convinced
that she must go to see it for herself.

When the *Gambler* got back, we went to Kidney Island to
collect our film and gear, and I picked some wild strawberries
for our friends at the Ship. That afternoon we made our way
through more wind and rain to the wireless station where Sewall
tape-recorded an interview on our experiences in the colony to
be broadcast over the radio. It gave him an opportunity to say
much that needed to be said about conservation measures. They
are resisted in the Falklands, as they are in so many places, even
the United States. Without sermonizing he questioned the de-
sirability of bounties on certain birds, and the unrestricted shooting
of birds just because they made good targets. He pointed out
the importance of sanctuaries such as Carcass Island, and suggested that farmers give some thought to the protection of upland
geese as a valuable food to supplement mutton. He believed that
the birds of the Falklands were among their greatest natural
assets—as long as they were kept alive.

At dinner that night we had the wild strawberries drenched
with cream and sugar. A young German dentist who had arrived
on the *Nigris N.* still was unable to speak much English; he
merely looked distressed. Other guests made unconvincing at-
tempts to show appreciation. Dr. Richter, the young German
tuberculosis specialist who had X-rayed Sewall's arm, was the
only frank one.

"I feel more pity for you than ever. Imagine having to eat
these." He wrinkled his nose and sniffed. "There is the distinct
flavor of peat."

Dr. Richter was elated over the conversion of the *Philomel* into a floating X-ray unit to go to every corner of the archipelago. The carpenters were working overtime and he expected the ship would be ready to start in two weeks. The three months' trip would take him to every sheep farm and settlement: he would take all the films and develop them and make diagnoses, and select the patients to be sent to the hospital in Stanley. The incidence of tuberculosis was high in the Falklands, and the islanders, it was predicted, would resist being X-rayed; but Dr. Richter's personality and enthusiasm seemed likely to overcome that.

"It will be one of the first floating units in the world," he said proudly. "It has been tried in Norway but not on such a scale."

The next day I went up to Grandma Davis's and found Agnes surrounded by several large suitcases and piles of merchandise.

"Come, help me pack," she said. "Huckle just phoned. We're leaving in an hour."

Everything had to be inspected—a clock, a saddle, yards of cloth, china, jumpers for the children, presents for everyone on New Island.

"Tony Felton's back with the *Overseas.* Got home yesterday safe and sound. My, Jack sounded relieved."

She threw things at the suitcases, I crammed them in, and we both sat on them. A car came to drive them to the jetty, and soon they were away to New Island in the Beaver.

Sewall and I went to the gentoo colony in the *Gambler,* dropping anchor in Sparrow Cove. We tried again to photograph the *Great Britain,* so desolate in her open grave. It was hard to imagine that bands had played and banners waved at her gala launching and that Queen Victoria had once trod her polished decks, now rusting and lined with roosting shags. The Falkland summer had not softened the grim outlines of Mount Lowe rising behind her, shrouded in rain and mist.

The gentoo colony on Arrow Point that we had first visited in October—ages ago—was deserted except for a few downy young and some bedraggled, molting adults. We thought all the other penguins had gone to the beach at Rabbit Cove until we noticed a couple of teen-agers disappearing over the edge of the bluff. We followed them and found others gingerly picking their way along the sheep paths down the rocky slope to the sea. Below us were the rest of the teenagers, wading and playing in the tidal pools among the surf-splashed rocks. Not an adult penguin was in sight.

From the lichen-covered ledges near the water we photographed the young birds' clumsy efforts to get into the water. Some were timid, testing the water with one foot, then the other; some were reckless and charged into the water splashing and often knocking down those that stood in the way. The gang spirit still prevailed. A group plunged into a tidal pool. They tipped each other over, tumbled about, rolled first on their bellies, then on their backs. With their flippers beating, some tried to porpoise even in the shallow pools. The older and more daring crept out on the rocks that dipped into the sea and waddled into the surf, then returned after a short swim. If they rested too close to the water, a wave was sure to sweep them seaward again. At times many birds gathered around Sewall and picked at his boots and tripod. When he shooed them away they plunged into the pools head first, feet first, with flippers waving.

Young gentoos, fascinated, explore the water

Young gentoos taking their first dip

No matter how they got into the water they were instantly at home. They had met the sea and recognized their element. Here they would live for the rest of their lives.

At midday, activity was at its height, but as the afternoon wore on, more and more penguins slowly gave up playing and climbed, stumbled, and scrambled back to the colony to which the adults were returning by the long path from the beach. By four, when the *Gambler* appeared and lay off the point, the rocks were almost deserted. We went aboard and from the deck watched the top of the bluff and the lively chasing that still ensued before the adults could be coaxed to give up throatfuls of food.

We had to visit the lighthouse and thank the keepers who had rescued us twice from Kidney Island. Mr. Goodwin's Land-Rover had at last succumbed to the Stanley roads; its battery was cracked, and there was not a spare in town. So he got Buzz Aldrich to take us.

Pembroke Light stood at the end of a rocky, sandy trail that sometimes nearly disappeared. The sea swirled around the rocks and feathery spindrift rose from the whitecaps. The two keepers, having spotted our car a long way off, met us at the door, and accepted our thanks with a casual graciousness, inviting us in to see the light. We climbed a circular staircase that wound around the inside of the tower to the glass enclosure that held the great oil-burning lamp. Every bit of metal shone from constant polishing, each pane of glass glistened, and all the other surfaces appeared to have been freshly painted.

We looked out from the tower through binoculars across Port William and the gray shoulder of Mount Lowe to a thin green line—Kidney Island.

"If Kidney Island were lower or Mount Lowe higher, we never would have seen the light from your torch," one keeper said. "We would have seen the flash, though. We thought you were trying out some new kind of rocket. At first I put a dark curtain up to change the timing of the light without stopping it. Did you notice?"

I had sensed a pause, but was looking for a colored light. I was so sure they couldn't stop or change the beam. They could, they said, but of course it would have to be entered in the log.

We went below to the tiny kitchen-dining room where the men took turns preparing meals, and had tea and homemade cakes for smoko. There were three keepers, they told us. Shifts of two weeks on duty and one week off kept two men there all the time. Lonesome? Goodness, no. There was more than enough work to keep them busy; in fact they hardly had time to read all the books and magazines that were sent to them.

Packing up to leave, I recalled all the pleasant moments, the frustrations, the mishaps, and the triumphs of our expedition. The story was all there in assorted items—blue jeans, faded, paper thin, and patched; jackets, stained and torn; a sling, its corners perforated from countless pinnings; cameras, no longer new; a Graflex, rusty from sea spray; rocks, scratched by penguin feet; earthworms and insects, preserved in bottles; old bones, a lambskin, pebbles, mosses, and postage stamps. It took us several days to pack it all; friends paused at the door to gape in dismay at the disorder within, and sniffed at the smell of preservatives. There were endless interruptions. By Friday, everything was ready;

we tied the packages, nailed the boxes, and summoned Buzz Aldrich to take them to the *Fitzroy*.

Then we had to think about money. It was a paradox. We had too much—an unusual dilemma for a college professor— and yet not enough. We had plenty of pounds which, because of currency restrictions, we could not convert into dollars. Sewall said he was too busy to bother about money and left it up to me.

In the office of the Colonial Treasurer I tried to formulate a plan for changing pounds into dollars without landing in jail. We had to stay in Montevideo for at least ten days—until all the luggage was in the air headed for the States. If, as he told me, we could only take five pounds each with us how were we going to live, and what would happen to the rest of the money?

He was friendly but firm. He would give us an allowance, limited but adequate—a few pounds for living expenses, a few pence for daily extravagances—for two weeks. The rest of the money would just have to stay in the Falklands.

My dreams of leather coats and alligator shoes vanished, not to mention the flight over the Andes to Chile and a visit to Buenos Aires. I went back to the hotel and vented my fury on Sewall. Of course I knew *why* there was an exchange barrier, but it was senseless. With all this talk of improving international relations, everything was done to keep people from going from one country to another; why were they not allowed unlimited opportunities to become acquainted. . . .

"Hold it," Sewall finally said grinning. Smug as the Carcass Island cat, he drew from his pocket a roll of bills—American money.

"Where . . . I thought you changed it all?"

"I kept some, just in case, in the bottom of the camera box under the lens paper." And he was too busy to bother about money!

I went to the F.I.C. to arrange for our allowance in Montevideo. After we had settled the account, I looked longingly at the tidy balance left to the credit of Walt Disney Productions. Someone in Hollywood was going to be very annoyed. On my way back to the hotel I passed a church. A painter, high up on a scaffolding, called to me and waved his brush. It was the young man from New York. He'd found a place to live, he said, and he still liked the Falklands. He'd be home in two years.

Sir Miles Clifford, Governor of the Falkland Islands, was re-
tiring and sailing on the *Fitzroy* with us. A capable and efficient
governor for seven years, he had done a great deal for the colony.
He was responsible for many improvements, particularly in the
health and education departments, and numerous innovations,
among them the system of wireless communication. Personally
we were indebted to him for arranging every possible aid for
our project.

Sewall and I took part in the festivities that preceded his
departure. The morning I got back, exhausted and hungry, from
Kidney Island, the first thing I noticed on entering my room was
an engraved invitation to dinner at Government House, white tie
and decorations and all, for that very night. I had been too tired
to do anything but laugh at the idea. Fortunately it had been
called off; the guests, mostly from the outlying farms, were unable
to get to Stanley because of the storm.

Finally, the week before we left, the two airplane pilots, using
both planes, had managed to have all the members of Legco
in town for the farewell session. On a sunny, windy morning
the Governor, in full dress uniform, reviewed the honor guard
in front of the Town Hall before opening the meeting of the
Legislative Council of the Falkland Islands in the name of Her
Majesty Queen Elizabeth II.

There was only a handful of onlookers. Two rows of blue-
uniformed guards stood at attention as the Governor, accompanied by his aide-de-camp, stepped from his black limousine
and strode stiffly up and down. The captain, sword in hand,
followed just one step behind. The wind snatched the cap off
one hapless guard and whirled it across the street where it caught
in a gorse hedge. When a sudden gust whipped fiercely at the
white ostrich plumes in the Governor's hat I expected it to
follow. The Colonial Secretary, in top hat, morning coat, and
striped trousers, advanced to meet the Governor and escort him
into the Hall.

In the afternoon the Governor had a cocktail party, in lieu
of the formal dinner, and people appeared from all corners of
the camp. Even Mr. Napier from West Point was on hand. He
assured us he had made the trip only because he had to see
the dentist. The manager of Bleaker Island, which we had missed,
urged us to make another visit, and the new magistrate of South

Georgia invited us to come to his rugged corner of sub-Antarctica.

When I went to the F.I.C. office to straighten out our accounts I had found Freddy White and Mr. Barton conferring over the ceremonies for the Governor's departure. I asked Freddy if we could stay on the jetty long enough to photograph the event and board the *Fitzroy* from a small boat after the Governor had left. He denied this small request so emphatically that it startled me.

"Sir Miles must be the last to leave Stanley. There's no question about that. You will go aboard at the F.I.C. jetty with the other passengers. We will then lay off Government Jetty where the Governor will board the *Philomel* and be brought out to us. Don't ask me why," he added, "that is the way it is done."

"As soon as the Governor is on the *Fitzroy* I'll take her up the harbor, turn, and come back past the town while the guns on the frigate give the salute. You can stay on the bridge and take pictures from there. Will you take movies with my camera? I'd like to have a record of the event, and I'll be too involved."

"Delighted," I said, "I'm especially good under fire."

"Which reminds me," said Mr. Barton, "if the frigate is not here, they'll have to use the guns in front of the hotel. Have you checked the ammunition?"

"The Colonial Secretary personally checked it this morning," Freddy said with a deadpan expression. "He will recheck on Tuesday morning." We all laughed, but not very heartily—we recalled the firing of the guns a month before. At that time the supposedly blank charges had raised great clouds of smoke and debris in the camp on the opposite side of the harbor. This time the *Fitzroy* would be in the direct line of fire.

"I hope the Colonial Secretary can be depended on," I said. "If we are to be on the bridge. . . ."

"Not to worry," Freddy said. "You fuss too much."

Not to worry. It had taken me five months to adopt the Falklanders' philosophy of accepting the inevitable with calm, of doing one thing at a time and enjoying it to the full, of facing problems when they came without anticipating them.

This serenity was somewhat ruffled on the morning of our departure. Even the usually calm F.I.C. agent wore a nervous frown as he hurried through breakfast. Was everything properly loaded on the *Fitzroy?* Had the right hatch been left open so the Governor's dress uniform could be stowed in the right trunk?

The departure went according to plan. Although there were heavy low-hanging clouds, the elements for once favored the Governor. We watched from the bridge as the official party walked slowly down the jetty past the honor guard and cluster of school children and paused to shake hands with the leading citizens. Then they boarded the *Philomel* which turned smartly toward the *Fitzroy*. As the Governor mounted the steps of the *Fitzroy* his official flag went up the mast.

Concealed behind wooden barricades we photographed His Excellency and his family as they waved their farewells. We could not wave, only gaze at the friends who had been so kind to us, and at the familiar landmarks that slid by so fast: the Battle Monument, the hospital, the Town Hall, the Ship Hotel, the Cathedral, the F.I.C. The guns on shore shattered the stillness with a salute.

Both airplanes swooped, circled, and dived over the *Fitzroy* again and again. John Huckle waved from the Auster, and I could imagine the grin on his face. All that was lacking was a salute from the frigate, but she had vanished in the night.

Halfway down Port William we leaned on the rail for a last look at the gentoos—the teenagers on the rocks, the adults on the beach. The buzzing planes upset them; many took to the water and swam about with their heads and tails held high as they often did when alarmed. Others stood still and stared.

Would we ever see them at home again, ever watch them porpoise in from the sea, lounge on the beach, or steal diddle-dee? We packed the tarnished cameras in their shabby cases. The *Philomel,* which had escorted us to the lighthouse, turned back with a final blast of her whistle, and the *Fitzroy* headed for the open sea.

Scientific Names of Animals and Plants

BIRDS

black-browed albatross	*Diomedea melanophris*
black-chinned siskin	*Spinus barbatus*
black and white oystercatcher	*Haematopus leucopodus*
black-crowned night heron	*Nycticorax nycticorax*
black oystercatcher	*Haematopus ater*
black-throated finch	*Melanodera melanodera*
blue-eyed shag	*Phalacrocorax albiventer*
brent goose	*Chloëphaga rubidiceps*
Cassin's tern	*Sterna hirundinacea*
Cape pigeon	*Daption capensis*
Chilean swallow	*Iridoprocne leucopyga*
Chiloë widgeon	*Anas sibilatrix*
Cobb's wren	*Troglodytes musculus*
correndera pipit	*Anthus correndera*
crested duck	*Lophonetta specularioide.*
dolphin gull	*Leucophaeus scoresbii*
Falkland flightless steamer duck	*Tachyeres brachypterus*
Falkland plover	*Charadrius falklandicus*
Falkland robin	*Turdus falcklandii*
firebird	*Pachyptila belcheri*
Fuegian oystercatcher	*Haematopus leucopodus*
gentoo penguin	*Pygoscelis papua*
giant fulmar	*Macronectes giganteus*
gray-backed petrel	*Garrodia nereis*
gray duck	*Lophonetta speculqrioides*
ground-tyrant	*Muscisaxicola macloviana*

house wren	*Troglodytes musculus*
jackass penguin	*Spheniscus magellanicus*
kelp gull	*Larus dominicanus*
kelp goose	*Chloëphaga hybrida*
king penguin	*Aptenodytes patagonicus*
king shag	*Phalacrocorax albiventer*
logger duck	*Tachyeres brachypterus*
macaroni penguin	*Eudyptes chrysolophus*
mollymawk	*Diomedea melanophris*
Paraguayan snipe	*Capella paraguaiae*
red-breasted troupial	*Pezites militaris*
rockhopper penguin	*Eudyptes crestatus*
rock shag	*Phalacrocorax magellanicus*
sheathbill	*Chionis alba*
shoemaker	*Procellaria aequinoctialis*
short-eared owl	*Asio flammeus*
skua	*Catharacta skua*
slender-billed whalebird	*Pachyptila belcheri*
sooty albatross	*Phoebetria fusca*
sooty shearwater	*Puffinus griseus*
stinker	*Macronectes giganteus*
turkey vulture	*Cathartes aura*
tussockbird	*Cinclodes antarcticus*
upland goose	*Chloëphaga picta*
winter plover	*Zonibyx modestus*
yellow-billed teal	*Anas flavirostris*

OTHER ANIMALS

aquatic beetles	*Dytiscus* sp.
blackfish	*Globicephala* sp.
fur seal	*Arctocephalus australis*
mullet	*Eleginops maclovinus*
mussels	*Mytilus edulis*
sea lion	*Otaria byronia*

shrimps	*Munida* sp.
wingless crickets	*Parudenus* sp.

Plants

balsam bog	*Azorella filamentosa*
cypress	*Cupressus macrocarpa*
dandelions	*Taraxacum* sp.
diddle-dee	*Empetrum rubrum*
English daisy	*Bellis perennis*
gorse	*Ulex europaeus*
evergreens	*Cupressus macrocarpa*
pale maidens	*Sisyrinchium filifolium*
pigberry	*Gunnera magellanica*
sand cabbage	*Leuceria suaveolens*
scurvy grass	*Oxalis enneaphylla*
tussock grass	*Poa flabellata*
veronica	*Veronica elliptica*
white grass	*Cortaderia* sp.
wild celery	*Apium graveolens*
wild strawberry	*Rubus geoides*
yellow flowers	*Senecio* sp.

Eleanor Pettingill